Simon & Schuster
Modular Science
Key Stage 4

Science Changes!

Peter Ellis

Acknowledgements
The author and publisher would like to thank the following for permission to reproduce photographs: Adrian Arbib, 1.2d; Associated Press, 3.6b; Austrian National Library, 2.3a; Bodleian Library, Oxford, 2.6a; Bridgeman Art Library, 2.1c; British Maritime Technology, 1.6c; J. Allan Cash, 2.4b, 2.5b; CEGB, 1.2c; CLEAR, 3.4b; Peter Ellis, 1.1a; Mary Evans, 2.5g; Hulton-Deutsch, 1.4e, 2.2d; IBM, 1.5d; ICCE, 3.1d; Rob Kendrick/University of Houston, 1.5b; Simon Kendal, 3.2b; Kew Gardens, 1.6a; Ander McIntyre, 1.1c, 3.4a; NASA, 3.5a, 3.5b, 3.5c, 3.5d; National Maritime Museum, 2.2b; National Portrait Gallery, 1.6b; Popperfoto, 2.6c; Ann Ronan, 1.3c, 2.4a, 2.4c; Royal Astronomical Society, 2.1a, 2.1b; Royal Geological Society, 3.6d; Royal Institution, 1.3a; Science Museum, 2.5c, 2.5d; Science Photo Library, cover (Lawrence Berkeley Laboratory/SPL), 1.2b, 1.5a, 2.5f, 3.1a, 3.1e; Siemens-Plessey, 1.1b; Topham, 3.2a; Weidenfeld and Nicolson Archive, 2.2c; Werner Forman Archive, 2.5e; WISE, 2.6b.

First published in 1992 in Great Britain by
Simon & Schuster Education
Campus 400, Maylands Avenue
Hemel Hempstead, Herts HP2 7EZ

British Library Cataloguing in Publication Data

Ellis, Peter
Science changes.
1. Science, history
I. Title
509
ISBN 0 7501 0179 2

The cover shows a demonstration of the Meissner effect.

Designed, typeset and illustrated by
VAP Publishing Services
Kidlington
Oxfordshire

Printed in Hong Kong by Wing King Tong Co. Ltd.

Key to icons used in text

word processor

safety goggles

CONTENTS

Changing Methods – How scientists work

Changing Views – How different races, governments, religions and society have viewed science and scientists

Changing Values – The uncertainty of scientific knowledge; cost versus benefit

1.1 A DAY IN THE LIFE OF A SCIENTIST

- What is it like being a scientist or an engineer? Is it like any other job or do you have to be something special?
- Is real science the same as the science you do in your school laboratory?

Science is about finding things out and explaining what you find; engineers apply these ideas to making something. If you really enjoy doing this in school science then it is likely that you will enjoy working as a scientist or an engineer. In this unit we look at the kind of things a scientist and an engineer do in an ordinary day.

NILLA KARLSSON

Nilla is Swedish and went to school and university in the ancient city of Uppsala. For the last year of her degree in biochemistry she moved to a British university and then stayed on to do research for a higher degree (a Ph.D.). As well as Swedish and English, she also speaks French and can converse with the other foreign scientists in her research group. She enjoys travelling and has only been home to Sweden briefly since arriving in England.

Nilla is a member of a large group working on glycosylation of proteins. The work is sponsored by a multinational drug company so Nilla finds that there is a good supply of equipment.

▲ **Nilla preparing a sample for electrophoresis**

Activity

Nilla's work involves a lot of chromatography. Perhaps you have carried out some experiments on chromatography yourself. If not, try this experiment in paper chromatography.

- What dyes are present in inks?

You will need: Strips of chromatography paper (approximately 2 cm × 15 cm), beaker or jar 10–15 cm tall, glass rod or pencil, felt-tip pens or coloured inks, ethanol.

Mark a strip of chromatography paper with a pencil line, 2 cm from the end of the strip. Place a drop of ink on this mark. Rest the glass rod on top of the beaker containing water. Hang the paper strip over the rod so that the paper just touches the surface of the liquid. Leave the beaker in a draught-free area for half an hour. Repeat the experiment with various inks and with ethanol instead of water, but try to make the conditions identical in each case. Let the paper strips dry, then cut them into 1 cm fragments (don't mix them up!). Examine each fragment and estimate the fraction of strip coloured by the ink dyes. For each of your experiments, plot a graph showing how much of each fragment of chromatography paper is dyed (y-axis), compared to its distance from the starting point (x-axis). Your graphs will look similar to some of the results that Nilla gets from her experiments.

Nilla's day

8.00 I am usually at my desk by 8.00 a.m. First, I check my diary for the day – there may be meetings or seminars to attend – and then make my final plans for the day's experiments. A chromatography experiment has been left running all night, so I check to see how it is getting on. I carry out some of my experiments with a colleague, so we talk about the progress we have made.

9.00 I move to the tissue culture room which is kept cool and is closed off from the rest of the laboratory. The cultures (animal cells that grow and multiply) are kept in a large incubator at a constant 37°C. I remove my sample and put it in a centrifuge to concentrate the cells. I take a tiny sample, dilute it and add a dye that colours the cells. I then examine a drop under a microscope and count the number of cells. I can tell from this whether or not the cells have multiplied sufficiently. I treat the remaining cells with an inhibitor and a radioactive 'label' and leave them for a few hours. Finally, I feed the other cultures in the incubator with nutrients.

10.30 Back to the main laboratory for a cup of coffee and a chat with colleagues. Most of the discussion is about work; I find that talking is one of the best ways of getting inspiration. Now it is time to stop the chromatography experiment that has been going overnight. The results aren't ready yet as they are invisible but slightly radioactive. I have to measure each fraction of the chromatogram using a scintillation counter – the radioactivity in the sample produces points of light which must be counted and then plotted onto a graph.

1.00 Sandwich time.

2.00 Back to the tissue culture room. The cells that I prepared in the morning are now ready for analysis. I place the cells in a centrifuge again and then treat them with detergents and other reagents to separate and break up the proteins. I then put the mixture on a gel for electrophoresis. Electrophoresis is similar to chromatography, but here a high voltage separates the different substances being analysed. I leave the electrophoresis experiment to run overnight.

3.00 It is time for this week's seminar. Each week, one of the workers in the group gives a talk about their work, followed by a discussion.

4.00 I now have to prepare another sample for chromatography and program the computer to maintain the necessary conditions overnight.

4.30 I start to plot the results from the scintillation counter. The graphs will tell me what sugars are present in my mixture and provide one more bit of data in my search for the structure of the complex sugars.

5.30 I write up my notebook. My notebook is important, because when I write up a paper, I will refer to it for details of every experiment that I have carried out.

6.00 It is time to go home – provided that none of my experiments have caused problems or the apparatus gone wrong!

Sugars and health

For many years, biochemists have been interested in proteins and DNA, while sugars have been thought to be unimportant and only sources of energy for animals and plants. Recently, however, it has been found that the action of some proteins is affected by sugar molecules attached to them. This is known as **glycosylation** of proteins.

Sugars consist of carbon, hydrogen and oxygen, and sometimes nitrogen. The atoms can join up in chains, rings and branches, and the task of working out the structure of a particular sugar is much more difficult than finding the structure of a protein or even DNA. A sugar molecule looks rather like a map of the motorways of Great Britain. Scientists have to snip off each bit of motorway between junctions to identify it. It is important to find the structure of these sugars as this promises to find the cause, and perhaps even a cure, for diseases such as sleeping sickness, rheumatoid arthritis and AIDS. Nilla's group uses enzymes to split up the sugars into smaller units for analysis.

Now try these

1 Why is keeping a notebook important?

2 Tissue cultures must be 'fed' every day. What problems do you think this causes Nilla?

3 Biochemistry is just one science, and Nilla's work just one part of that. Find out what research is being done in other sciences.

4 Nilla's work is pure science – she is trying to find out something no-one knows already. Eventually, applied scientists may be able to use Nilla's work to produce new drugs. Why is pure scientific research important?

1.1 A DAY IN THE LIFE OF A SCIENTIST

Martin Bartlett – Engineer

▲ **Martin testing a pcb**

8.30 I am already at my desk in the open-plan 'Digital Techniques' office. I have been asked to find and correct a fault in a pcb that I have designed. The pcb was supposed to remove the 'clutter' (the fixed objects) from a radar picture, but when it was tested in a simulator, an error was found. I examine the pages of circuit diagrams and find the cause of the error.

9.15 I go to the computer room at the end of the office. Air-conditioned and cool, the room contains approximately 20 net-worked micro-computers of various types. Using one of them, I call up the stored information on the circuit of the pcb which gives me details of each component that was used.

9.30 A short walk takes me to the Electrical Computer-Aided Design department where more computers are used to arrange the wiring of components on the pcbs. I discuss the problem with a colleague and after a short delay, call up the detailed circuit diagram on the computer. I can now find the precise points where changes have to be made.

Activity

There are many different types of engineering. Collect some newspapers and magazines that carry adverts offering jobs to engineers.
Make a list of the companies and organisations that advertise the engineering jobs, the type of engineer required and any other information given (eg qualifications required, salary).

- What type of engineer is most in demand?
- Do companies need different types of engineer?

MARTIN BARTLETT

Martin Bartlett is 23 and is keen on basketball and motorbikes. He became interested in electronics while at school and when he left after his O' levels (the forerunners of GCSE), Plessey Radar Ltd. took him on as an apprentice. Four years later, after gaining experience in many areas of the company's work and a Higher National Certificate from the local college, he asked if the company would sponsor him to get a degree. The company was pleased to do this and Martin went to polytechnic. Two years later he completed a degree in Electronic Engineering. He has now been back at the company (now known as Siemens-Plessey Radar Ltd.) for a year.

Most of Martin's colleagues went to university or polytechnic after completing the sixth form at school, but he is pleased with his additional experience of working. In fact, he has been in the company longer than some of his bosses. Martin is part of a team of five led by Adrian Steel who, along with a number of other Project leaders, reports to Peter McKnight, the Manager of part of the Design Engineering section.

The company designs and builds radar systems for military and civil applications. Martin's team designs the electronic circuitry that sends out, receives and interprets radar signals. The circuitry is built up from a number of large printed circuit boards (pcbs).

Martin spends some days with a pencil, paper and data books, designing a pcb for a new radar system. The day he describes illustrates the different aspects of his work.

10.00 Back at my desk, I finalise my plans. The wiring has to be changed and one of the micro-processors on the pcb has to be reprogrammed.

10.10 Into the computer room to a different computer which is linked to a processor programming machine. I type in the new program and the computer runs a check to test for errors. At first, there are a lot of mistakes, but gradually I correct them all.

11.40 Now that the program is complete, it is time for a cup of tea.

11.45 I take the pcb to the electronics laboratory – some of the components have to be removed and the wiring changed. Meanwhile, a colleague asks for help with the programming of one of the computers. Thanks to my apprenticeship, I have had a lot of experience with the computing systems in my department.

12.45 Lunch in the company cafeteria – there's quite a choice – and a chance for a chat, and to read.

1.30 Back to work in the computer room to reprogram the micro-processor.

1.45 The processor is taken to the laboratory for fitting to the pcb and the wiring to be completed. Adrian Steel, my boss, calls by to check progress and also to ask me to solve another problem with the radar system. With the revised pcb now complete, I test the new circuits with a meter and leave the whole pcb to be tested later.

2.15 Back to the computer room to look at the new problem. This concerns the 'back plane' that connects the pcbs together. A problem arises; I can't get into the computer. The computing managers have changed the authorisation codes and the computer won't recognise me. A few minutes pass as the mistake is corrected. At last I am able to call up the detailed wiring diagram of the back plane. I find the source of most of the problems, but the others stubbornly remain. I telephone Richard, the computing expert who had found the errors, and realise that there has been some confusion in the computing software. Adrian Steel calls in and we discuss the problem. Richard brings details of the program and we work through the errors together. Finally, I am left alone to complete the corrections.

3.30 It's tea-time. I chat with Adrian and some other colleagues.

4.00 Back to the computer room to complete the back plane problem.

4.20 There's time for one last job. A set of micro-processors must be programmed for fitting to a pcb. I call up the relevant program on the computer, check it against the circuit details, program each processor and record what I have done.

4.45 The day is over, but I am not quite finished. A few more minutes' work and then it's home. No overtime today.

▲ **A Siemens-Plessey radar in action**

Now try these

1 Martin says that the part of his job he enjoys the most is when he uses pencil and paper to create new circuits. Why do you think he feels this?

2 Martin has computing skills and practical electronic skills, as well as a good scientific understanding of his subject. What scientific skills did he show in his day's work?

3 Martin is at the start of his career. Later, he will spend more time managing a team or a whole department. What skills will he have to learn?

4 Electronics is not everybody's favourite subject. Choose one area of science that you have studied and describe how it is used to benefit people.

1.2 WHAT GOES UP MUST COME DOWN

When a ball is thrown in the air, you expect it to fall to the ground. Why?

Isaac Newton's Theory of Gravitation gives us a method to work out what will happen when a ball is thrown. It predicts when and where the ball will land, provided we know a few facts about the force with which the ball was thrown. Usually, however, you do not need to carry out complicated calculations to make a prediction. You base your judgement on what has happened every other time that you have thrown a ball. You generalise and say that whenever a ball is thrown up it will eventually fall to Earth.

Generalisation and **prediction** are very important in science. Scientists perform experiments to produce results which can be repeated over and over again. The scientist then produces a generalisation which is often called a 'law'. However, a scientist can never be completely sure that the law is correct. For example, if you threw a ball hard enough it wouldn't fall back to Earth but go into orbit or escape from the Earth's atmosphere. The simple law 'what goes up must come down' doesn't allow for the possibility of orbiting satellites. Newton's theory does. Scientists test theories by making predictions. If the predictions prove to be correct then the theory must be at least partly true.

Activity

To answer the following questions, you can **either** carry out the experiment a number of times to make a generalisation **or** you can start with a theory and predict what might happen.

1 How does the heat produced by a wire change when the voltage across it is increased?

You will need: Power pack, voltmeter, leads, coil of wire or immersion heater, beaker, thermometer, measuring cylinder.

2 How does the concentration of an acid affect the rate at which a metal reacts with it?

You will need: An acid (eg hydrochloric acid), a reactive metal (eg magnesium ribbon), beaker, measuring cylinder, stopwatch.

- What are the variables?
- Which variables must be kept constant. Which should be changed?

Before you start your experiments write down a brief description of what you think will happen (a theory) and predict an answer to the questions. Is your prediction correct? Alternatively, you could carry out the experiments a number of times. Can you write out a statement that is a generalisation of your results (a law)?

Some scientific generalisations

- Penicillium mould kills bacteria.
- White light entering a prism emerges coloured red orange yellow green blue indigo violet.

▲ **Where does the colour come from?**

- Acids turn methyl orange pink.
- People suffer from hayfever more in hot, dry weather.
- The length of a spring will increase uniformly as the load on it is increased.
- All the alkali metals (Group 1) have a valency (oxidation number) of 1 in their compounds.

Metals conduct electricity

We recognise metals by their malleability, their shininess and their ability to conduct electricity. The latter property was first discovered by the English physicist, Stephen Gray (1666–1736). He was experimenting with static electricity and found that an electric charge disappeared if the charged object was supported by brass. He experimented with a variety of substances and finally decided that all the known metals (iron, copper, tin, lead, etc) conducted, while other substances (eg silk, paper) were insulators. From this it was simple to generalise that all metals must be conductors.

What theory supports this law? We think that substances will conduct electricity if electrons are only loosely attached to atoms and hence can pass from one atom to another. This theory of electrical conductivity has developed during the twentieth century.

Is the generalisation correct? Certainly all metals are conductors but the theory predicts that *any* substance with 'free' electrons will conduct. Today, scientists have made various ceramics and polymers which also conduct.

- Why is the statement 'all metals are conductors' useful to chemists?

▲ **A use for metal conductors**

As alike as two peas . . .

The founder of the science of genetics was the monk, Gregor Mendel (1822–84). He failed his exams to become a teacher and settled down to study plant breeding. Over a period of ten years he experimented with pea plants, carefully pollinating the flowers of one plant with pollen from another. From his results he was able to make a number of generalisations that became the laws of genetics. However, Mendel had no theory to explain his work and because he did not publish his results widely they were ignored for 16 years after his death. Only in the last 50 years, with the discovery of the structure of DNA and the properties of genes, has an explanation for Mendel's laws been possible. Now scientists are able to transfer genes from one plant to another to produce new varieties with predictable characteristics that Mendel could not have dreamt of.

All acids contain oxygen

Sometimes a generalisation can hinder instead of help a scientific discovery. Antoine Lavoisier, who devised the oxygen theory of combustion, burned many substances in oxygen and found that the oxides produced were acids. From this he made the step towards saying that all acids must contain oxygen. However, hydrochloric acid only contains hydrogen and chlorine, and it was many years before Humphry Davy finally proved that chlorine was not a compound of something with oxygen.

- What other acidic compounds do not contain oxygen?

Now try these

1 If the winter sky is clear the night will be frosty. Devise a theory that could predict this generalisation.

2 Choose two of the generalisations given in this unit and provide an explanation based on scientific theories.

3 What other generalisations do we make every day without a theory to justify our prediction? Are the generalisations usually accurate (eg red sky at night, shepherd's delight!)?

▲ **A sign of good weather?**

1.3 A MODEL SCIENTIST

The way science is done has changed considerably over the last two hundred years. Instead of men, often rich, working alone, we now have teams of scientists employed by industries, universities and governments. Nevertheless, science still demands the same skills of observation, inspiration and experimental technique. One scientist who showed all these skills was Michael Faraday. For the first half of the nineteenth century he dominated science in England and the work he did in physics and chemistry is still of great interest to scientists today. Faraday's methods of working provide a model which is worth copying by any of today's scientists.

The activities in this unit are copies of two experiments that Faraday used in his investigations of electricity (with slight modifications).

The life of a scientist

Michael Faraday had a poor childhood and little education. His parents were caring, but because of ill health were short of money. They were members of a small Christian sect called the Sandemanians who avoided much contact with non-members and preferred simple lives. In 1804, at the age of 13, Faraday began work as an errand boy for a bookseller, Mr Riebau, in London and the following year was apprenticed as a bookbinder. He read widely, attended philosophical lectures and made friends. He found out about the discoveries of Humphry Davy and began his own simple investigations into electricity.

In 1812, Faraday received tickets to attend lectures by Davy at the Royal Institution. He was fired with enthusiasm and determined to take up a career in science. He sent a bound copy of his lecture notes to Davy who had injured himself and needed an assistant. So in 1813 Faraday began his long association with the Royal Institution. Davy was a good teacher and gave Faraday every encouragement with his experiments. Davy took his young assistant on tours of Europe visiting scientists and this developed his knowledge of science. In 1821 Faraday was married to Sarah, another Sandemanian. Sarah was not trained in science, but encouraged Michael in his work. They had no children, but led a happy life together.

Faraday continued to progress at the Royal Institution. In 1824 he began lecturing and in 1826 started the Christmas lectures for children that still continue today. Also in 1826 he was appointed Director of the Laboratories, a position he held until his retirement in 1861. He worked tirelessly apart from a period between 1839 and 1845 when he suffered a strange mental illness.

Activity

The first electric motor (1821)

You will need: A small bar magnet, a foil cake tray, aluminium foil, two pieces of stiff copper wire (one long, one short), leads, crocodile clips, d.c. power pack, Plasticine, salt solution.

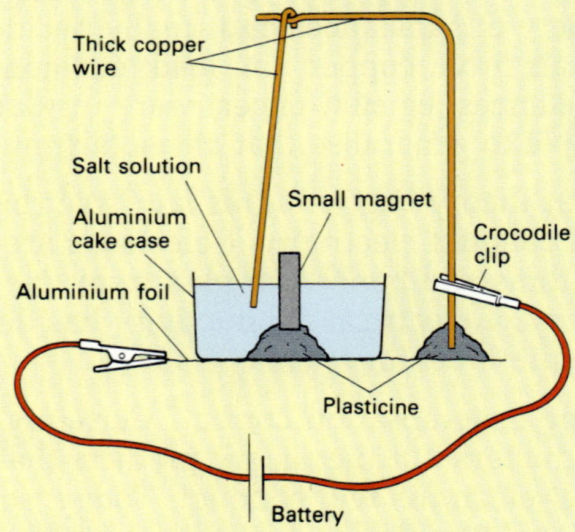

Set up the apparatus as shown in the diagram. The hanging wire should be suspended from the frame and be free to move. Turn on the power.

- What is the purpose of the salt solution (originally, Faraday used mercury)?
- What happens if you reverse the leads at the power pack?
- Try to explain what is happening in terms of the electric current and magnetic field.

Activity

The discovery of electromagnetic induction (1830)

You will need: d.c. power pack and leads, a galvanometer (a very sensitive meter), an iron ring (a washer will do), thin insulated copper wire.

Wind two lengths of copper wire around the ring, one on one side and one on the other. Connect one coil of wire to the power pack and the other to the galvanometer. Turn on the power and watch the meter.

- What do you see when the power is switched on and when it is switched off? Explain what is happening.

A scientist at work

Faraday's earliest work at the Royal Institution was as an analytical chemist. He learnt all the necessary techniques and became a highly skilled analyst in great demand. As he had done since his days as a bookbinder, Faraday recorded all his experiments and observations in neat handwriting in a laboratory diary. In 1825 he was sent a liquid to analyse from which he obtained a new substance - benzene. With typical thoroughness he carried out many tests on the substance to determine as many of its properties as possible and found its formula to be C_6H_6.

▲ **Faraday at work in the laboratory of the Royal Institution**

His interest gradually turned to electricity. Although he was constantly being asked to investigate a variety of problems brought to him by industrialists and the government, it was the investigation of the effects of electric current which occupied most of his working life. Faraday knew of the work of Ampère, Arago, Öersted, Wollaston and many others. He saw possibilities that others missed and he took Öersted's ideas of electric rotations to produce the first electric motor.

For years he searched for a way to use magnetism to produce electricity. He succeeded in 1830 only because his observational skills noted the small movement of the meter when a coil was connected to a battery. From his discovery of electromagnetic induction he built up a theoretical picture of magnetic and electric fields. When he went on to investigate the chemical effects of electricity, a completely new set of words was needed to explain what was occurring and with the help of Reverend William Whewell he came up with the terms anode, cathode, ion, cation, anion, etc.

There is no doubt that Faraday's careful experimentation and clearly thought-out theories were a great influence on the science of electricity and hastened the use of electricity in industry.

HANS ÖERSTED
1777–1851

Hans studied at the University of Copenhagen and after a period travelling around Europe as a journalist, returned there as Professor of physics. His most famous discovery was made in 1820 when he found that an electric current in a wire produces a magnetic field and will affect a compass.

ANDRÉ AMPÈRE
1775–1836

André had a troubled life with his father guillotined in the French revolution, the death of his first wife on the birth of his son and a troubled second marriage. However as Inspector-General of Universities he had a productive scientific career. In 1820 Öersted's discovery led him to show that two wires side-by-side carrying a current were attracted together, and he developed the first galvanometer which Faraday found so useful.

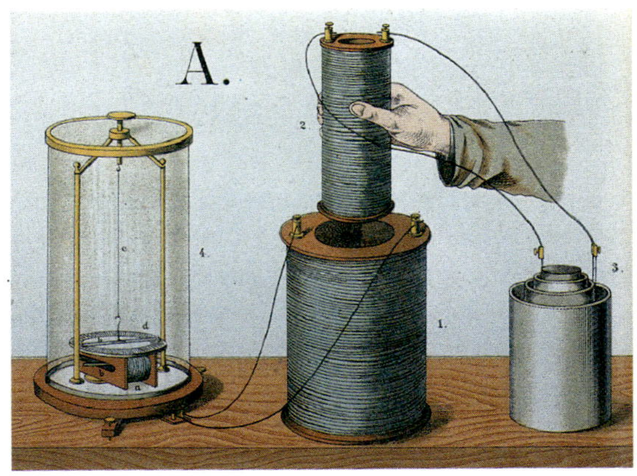

▲ **Faraday's induction machine**

Now try these

1. Why was keeping a laboratory diary important to Faraday?
2. Why are good experimental skills necessary for a good scientist?
3. What use was made of Faraday's discovery of electromagnetic induction?

1.4 THE HUNT FOR THE HELIX

Occasionally in science a discovery is made that completely alters the direction of scientific research and brings a new understanding in scientists' quests to find out how the Universe works. Sometimes these discoveries become widely known to people who have little knowledge of science at all. The discovery of the double helix of DNA was one of those discoveries. Like many examples of modern science, the discovery was the work of a large group of scientists although the names of Francis Crick and James Watson are the most familiar. The scientists involved were of all ages and from different parts of the world, and they had different personalities which affected the way they worked and the contribution they made to the discovery.

▲ **Crick and Watson and their model of DNA**

Activity

■ How do you solve problems?

There is always more than one way to get at the correct answer.

In a group of three, play a game of hangman. One member of the group should choose a fairly long word – a name of a place, a person or a pop group, for example. That person should write down a dash for each letter in the word and give a clue. Another person should suggest letters that may be in the word, until they are certain what the word is, while the other should just guess at words that would fit. Take it in turns to be the word chooser, the one that suggests letters and the guesser.

Once you have played the game a few times, stop and think about what has happened. Who won the most games – the one that suggests letters or the guesser? Did one help the other at all? How was the guesser able to get the right answer – pure luck or was there another factor that led them to the answer?

X-ray crystallography

If you look at a light through a thin piece of cloth you may see a pattern of bright spots – the light has been **diffracted** by the threads. Similarly, a pattern appears when X-rays pass through a crystal. This pattern is more complicated, though, because the atoms are arranged in a three-dimensional lattice. In X-ray crystallography, a beam of X-rays is directed at a crystal and the path of the diffracted rays is recorded on photographic film. When developed, the film shows a pattern of spots which is determined by the arrangement of atoms in the crystal. A simple crystal like sodium chloride gives a fairly simple pattern, while a complex molecule like a protein is extremely difficult to analyse. Computers are now used to analyse X-ray photographs and produce a 'map' of the molecule. X-ray crystallography was developed by William Bragg and his son Lawrence. Lawrence was Director of the Cavendish laboratories at Cambridge University from 1938 to 1954.

The plot

In the 1930s and 1940s it slowly became clear that deoxyribonucleic acid (DNA) carried the genes which somehow acted to determine the development of all living things. This had become clear from work on viruses. In 1951, Linus Pauling showed that proteins were able to coil up into a helical shape. Maurice Wilkins and his assistant Rosalind Franklin were using X-ray crystallography to try to work out the shape of the complex DNA molecule. It was difficult to get pure DNA to work on and even more difficult to get it to crystallise. However, Franklin eventually managed to get good X-ray photographs and began the laborious process of working out the positions of the atoms in the molecule. Meanwhile, Crick and Watson had become

The cast

MAX PERUTZ
Born: Vienna, 1914.

Studied chemistry at Vienna University. Moved to Cambridge, 1936. Determined the structure of haemoglobin by X-ray crystallography. Awarded Nobel Prize in 1962.

Personality: A respected leader of a large team.

FRANCIS CRICK
Born: Northampton, 1916.

Studied physics, London University. Worked on radar and mines in World War II. Afterwards worked on biology. Joined Max Perutz's group at Cambridge using X-ray crystallography to investigate large molecules in cells.

Personality: An imaginative theorist eager to solve problems produced by other scientists' experimental results.

LINUS PAULING
Born: Oregon, USA, 1901.

Ph.D. at California Institute of Technology, 1925. Produced theories of chemical bonding for which he was awarded Nobel Prize in 1954. Turned to shapes of molecules found in cells in the late 1940s.

Personality: Highly imaginative, but dismissive of other people's ideas; proud of his position as one of the great chemists of the twentieth century.

MAURICE WILKINS
Born: New Zealand, 1916.

Moved to Birmingham, 1922. Studied physics at Cambridge University. Worked on radar and the atomic bomb project. Disillusioned, turned to biological applications of physics. 1946, King's College London, started to investigate X-ray pattern of DNA.

Personality: Worked slowly; reluctant to jump to conclusions.

JAMES WATSON
Born: Chicago, 1928.

Studied zoology and behaviour of viruses. Moved to Copenhagen, 1950, to study biochemistry. Excited by possibility of finding structure of DNA using X-ray crystallography. Arranged for move to Perutz's group in 1951.

Personality: Fine memory and imagination, but little knowledge of chemistry or crystallography.

ROSALIND FRANKLIN
Born: 1920.

Educated in London and Cambridge. Joined Wilkins as expert in X-ray crystallography. One of very small number of women scientists.

Personality: excellent experimenter, very methodical in her approach to problems, rather unimaginative and secretive. Cold relationship with Wilkins and other male scientists. Died of cancer in 1958.

excited by the prospect of working out the structure of DNA and realised the value of Pauling's method of building scale models of molecules to reveal how the atoms could join together. They knew that Wilkins and Franklin's X-ray photographs would be of help but were afraid to interfere in the London pair's work. Nevertheless, hints provided by Wilkins gave Crick and Watson the information they needed to start building models; information about the chemical composition of DNA gave them the final clue.

The climax

Maurice Wilkins and Rosalind Franklin's X-ray photographs suggested that the DNA molecule was made up of a helix similar to Pauling's protein. But how many strands were there to the helical thread, two or three? In 1951, Crick and Watson fiddled with their model atoms and came up with a three-strand helix. They announced it to Perutz and Bragg with glee, but a mistake in their model was pointed out to them. During 1952, they occasionally got more information out of Wilkins. Early in 1953 came the news that Pauling had found the answer - a three-strand helix. At first Crick and Watson felt demoralised, but when they read Pauling's report they realised that he too had made a chemical error. Now they urgently sought help from Wilkins and began modelling in earnest. Franklin's work was slowly providing the answers. Two strands were needed and at last they realised that they were held together by weak bonds. They beat Wilkins and Franklin to the final answer - **the double helix** - by just a few days. Watson, Crick and Wilkins were awarded the Nobel prize in 1962.

Now try these

1. Why was it important for Wilkins to obtain a pure sample of DNA?
2. Franklin thought that model building would not provide an answer but calculating the structure from the X-ray photographs eventually would. What differences were there between the personalities of the people who used the two techniques?
3. Despite being a great chemist, Pauling made a mistake. How can mistakes sometimes be useful?
4. Read James Watson's account of the structure of DNA in his book *The double helix*.

1.5 GETTING WARMER

Science is usually a slow process of gaining knowledge from experiments being carried out in laboratories all over the world. Sometimes, but very rarely, a discovery is announced that fires the imagination of scientists everywhere and a burst of activity occurs. One such occasion was in 1986–87 after Alex Müller and Georg Bednorz announced a new type of superconductor.

Superconductors – discovery and disillusion

A superconducting material has no electrical resistance – a current will flow in a loop of superconducting wire for ever. It also has the property of repelling a magnetic field; this is called the **Meissner effect**.

▲ **A demonstration of the Meissner effect**

Superconductivity was discovered in 1911 by a Dutch physicist, Kamerlingh Onnes. He found that mercury loses its resistance when it is cooled to about 4 K (−269 °C). Over the years a number of other metals, mainly alloys containing the metal niobium, were found to be superconducting. By 1973, the highest temperature at which a material was superconducting was still only about 23 K (−250 °C). To cool a material to this temperature it must be placed in liquid hydrogen – a very dangerous liquid – or liquid helium at 4 K which is very expensive. For years, no further progress was made and scientists became disillusioned. However, engineers were investigating uses for superconductors in computers, levitated trains, the transmission of electricity and the magnets for body scanners.

A new material

Alex Müller had been working on superconductivity for years at Zurich University and at IBM's research laboratory in Zurich. He had decided that there was no point in experimenting on metals any further, so he started to

Activity

It is rare that an experiment in modern science can be done in a school laboratory but with a little extra equipment and a lot of care, you too can be involved in the search for high-temperature superconductors. Your teacher must supervise your work.

You will need: 1.13 g yttrium oxide, 3.95 g barium carbonate, 2.39 g copper(II) oxide, a pestle and mortar, a kiln (try the pottery room), a pellet die press (try your CDT workshop), a large magnet, plastic tweezers, liquid nitrogen (obtainable from a university or hospital).

Mix the yttrium oxide, barium carbonate and copper oxide and grind it together using the pestle and mortar, as finely as possible (**barium compounds are poisonous – do not swallow any**). Place the mixture in a kiln at 950 °C for nine hours. Grind the mixture up again and then compress it into a pellet. Put the pellet back into the kiln for another nine hours and then let it cool very slowly. To test your material, tie the pellet to a piece of cotton then cool it in liquid nitrogen (this is extremely cold – **do not get any on your skin**). Hang the pellet near the pole of a magnet. If it is superconducting then the pellet should be repelled by the magnet.

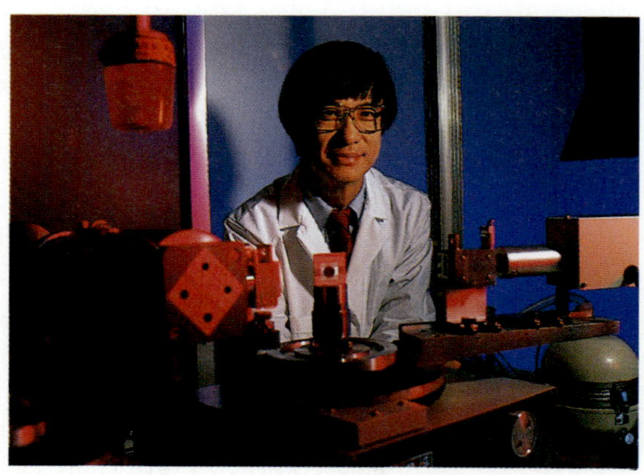

▲ **Paul Chu**

consider metal oxides. Most oxides are not conductors at all but some seemed to have metallic properties. As a respected scientist, Müller was able to follow his own ideas even if they weren't along the lines that IBM were interested in. In 1982, Georg Bednorz started to help Müller although he was employed by IBM on other research. In late 1985, they heard about some strange mixtures of copper oxide and other oxides that had some metallic properties and they started to investigate them. In February, they found a mixture of barium, lanthanum and copper oxides that superconducted at 30 K - a great increase. They continued to test the material and finally published their results in September 1986.

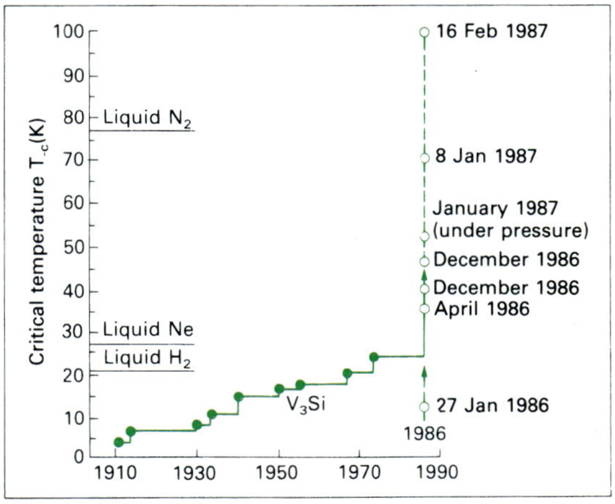

▲ **Discoveries in superconductivity**

The rush begins

Müller and Bednorz had found a completely new group of superconducting materials. Physicists and chemists read their paper and immediately set to work to investigate the properties for themselves. At IBM's research laboratories at Almaden, California and in New York they worked night and day. In Japan, scientists moved their beds into laboratories so that they did not have to leave their work. S. Tanaka at Tokyo found a material that superconducted at 40 K. Then in February 1987, Paul Chu at the University of Houston announced that a mixture of yttrium, barium and copper oxides superconducted at 90 K. Almost simultaneously, Zhao Zhongxian at the Institute of Physics, Beijing, reported a similar result. These were very important discoveries because now the material could be cooled in liquid nitrogen at 77 K. Liquid nitrogen is safe and cheap and frequently used by scientists to cool apparatus.

▲ **Müller and Bednorz**

Just a small meeting of physicists

The American Physical Society held its annual meeting in New York in March, 1987. The programme had been arranged months before but after Chu's announcement it was decided to add a short evening discussion. Five thousand people met that night and the meeting lasted from 7 pm to 6 am the following morning. The scientists felt an excitement like that experienced at a huge pop festival, as reports of discoveries were shared and ideas discussed.

After the meeting, researchers all over the world worked non-stop to find yet more new materials with even higher superconducting temperatures. In Budapest, Istvan Kirshner made a material that superconducted at 101 K and soon many groups were reporting superconductivity at 125 K.

In October 1987, Müller and Bednorz were awarded the Nobel Prize for Physics. Usually scientists have to wait ten years or more before being awarded the prize. This shows what a remarkable contribution their discovery of the new materials had made to the science of superconductors.

Now try these

1. In February and March 1987, many groups started to research high-temperature superconductors. Why do you think this was?
2. Apart from groups at universities, many industrial research laboratories (eg IBM, Toshiba, Bell) were also involved in the work on superconductors. Why was industry so involved with the research?
3. Some groups have reported superconductivity at room temperature and above but others have been unable to repeat these results. Why is it important to be able to repeat results in different laboratories?
4. Why do you think Bednorz and Müller were awarded the Nobel prize so quickly?
5. What differences are there between the discovery of 'high-temperature' superconductors and Faraday's discovery of electromagnetic induction?

1.6 CENTRES OF EXCELLENCE

Today it is usual to read of scientific developments being made by large teams of researchers working at universities, companies or government research establishments such as the Atomic Energy Research Establishment at Harwell, Oxfordshire or the Agricultural Research Establishment at Rothampstead, Hertfordshire. Every country now has its centres of excellence and governments and industry contribute millions of pounds to scientific research. There are also international centres, such as the CERN laboratory, which carries out research into the structure of matter for European governments. But government involvement in science has not always been so important.

The first moves to organised research, in Europe at least, were made by the Royal Society in England and the Academie des Sciences in France during the seventeenth century. Educated and well-to-do gentlemen met to discuss their discoveries and to suggest new lines of research. During the eighteenth century, governments started to become interested in science and engineering as new industries started. Overseas trade brought news of more and more strange plants and animals. However, it wasn't until the mid-nineteenth century that universities began to teach science and to set up their own research laboratories.

In the nineteenth century, two separate establishments were set up close together in south-west London. Both contributed a great deal to science in widely different fields.

Plants for living

The Royal Botanic Gardens at Kew are now a popular tourist attraction and indeed the plant houses are laid out to provide information for visitors. Nevertheless, the gardens continue with their original purpose of cataloguing and investigating plants found all over the world.

▲ **The computer-controlled Princess of Wales House at Kew**

SIR JOSEPH BANKS
1743–1820

▲ **Sir Joseph Banks in 1820**

Banks was educated at Eton and Oxford University where he studied classics. However, he was far more interested in plants. In 1764, he inherited his father's fortune and devoted his life to science. He sailed to Newfoundland and then to the South Pacific with Captain Cook as the expedition's botanist. He discovered many new plants which he brought back to England. Botany Bay in Australia was named by Captain Cook because of Banks' work. Back home, Banks became friends with King George III and advised him on the development of Kew. He became President of the Royal Society in 1772 and guided the institution until 1814. It was Banks who suggested setting up a colony at Botany Bay.

JOSEPH HOOKER
1817-1911

Hooker studied medicine at Glasgow before travelling on an expedition to the Antarctic in 1839 with Captain James Ross. He became interested in botany and later went to study the plants in the Himalayas. In 1865, he followed his father as Director of Kew Gardens. He made many improvements. When his friend, T. J. Phillips Jodrell died in 1876 and left a bequest to Kew, Hooker set up the Jodrell Laboratory to study the structure of plants. During Hooker's time, Kew became an important centre for the distribution of crop plants such as rubber, coffee, the oil palm, and many others.

The gardens were started by the Princess of Wales in 1759 on the estate owned by Frederick, her husband, who died in 1751. The gardens grew and during the reign of George III, Sir Joseph Banks helped to establish them as a centre for botanical research. In 1841, the government took over the running of the gardens and the Royal family gave more land. Sir William Hooker and his son Joseph, the first two directors, built up the scientific expertise of the staff at the gardens. At Kew today, students are trained in horticulture, the collections of plants are maintained and research is carried out in plant biology.

Testing standards

Towards the end of the nineteenth century a familiar situation had developed in science in Britain. Politically, the British Empire was at its height and British industry apparently led the world. However, some people were worried about the state of science and engineering. In 1883, a lavishly funded research establishment was set up in Berlin by the German government, but nothing like it existed in Britain. By 1914, 3000 German scientists were engaged in research for industry while there was little assistance for British companies. Nevertheless, some British scientists felt that there should be a national laboratory to carry out engineering tests and maintain standards of units and in 1900 the National Physical Laboratory (NPL) came into being under the directorship of Richard Glazebrook. The NPL was sited at Bushy House, a royal estate on the Thames, converted at a cost of £19000 to the government.

The NPL soon started its work of establishing standards, measuring the output of light bulbs, measuring the melting point of platinum (a standard temperature) and electric currents. The testing work also began; scientists investigated the effects of wind on structures, the properties of copper and aluminium alloys and the ability of various road surfaces to stand up to the wear and tear of vehicles. In 1910, the first ship-testing tank was built. Tank 1, 150 m long by 9 m wide, was used to find the best shapes for ships under various sea conditions. During World War I, aircraft became important and in 1915 a wind tunnel was built to carry out research in aerodynamics.

The NPL continues to carry out research in all branches of science and technology.

▲ **Testing models of ships' hulls at the NPL**

Activity

Maintaining standards

All the units used by scientists have to be measured against a **standard** which is maintained by organisations like the National Physical Laboratory. Instruments have to be **calibrated** to ensure that they are consistent with the accepted standard units.

Problem: Design, build and calibrate a simple balance to measure the mass of an object using a single standard mass (1 g, 100 g or 1 kg).

- Is your balance to be used for large (more than 10 g) or small (less than 10 g) masses?

You will need: Straws, string, pins, paper, strips of wood, sand, any other available materials that you think you need.

- How do you ensure your balance is calibrated correctly?

RICHARD GLAZEBOOK
1854–1935

Glazebook was born in Liverpool and became a lecturer in Mathematics at Cambridge University. In 1898 he was appointed Principal of University College Liverpool but soon left to become Director of the NPL. He guided the NPL through its first 19 years, often having to fight for extra staff, buildings and money to allow the work to continue.

Now try these

1. Why is the work of Kew Gardens in cataloguing and growing plants from all over the world important today?
2. What plant products do we use today that are cultivated as a result of the overseas expeditions of the last few hundred years?
3. Why do scientists need standards?
4. Why do you think industry found the NPL useful?
5. Should governments pay for scientific research or should the money come from other sources? Explain your answer.

2.1 AND YET IT MOVES!

> *'Joshua spoke with the Lord, and he said in the presence of Israel, "Stand still, O Sun, in Gibeon; stand still, Moon, in the Vale of Aijalon." So the sun stood still, and the moon halted.'*
> (*The Bible*, Joshua, chapter 10, verses 12-13)

Joshua's miracle was one passage in the Bible that was interpreted by Christian scholars as supporting the idea that the Earth was the unmoving centre of the Universe. Galileo was one of the few scholars who, at the beginning of the seventeenth century, questioned this view. When he was an old man, the Roman Catholic Church brought Galileo to trial. What was the argument all about?

Opposing theories

Aristotle, the third-century BC astronomer, put forward the theory that the Earth was fixed at the centre of the Universe with the Sun, Moon and stars revolving around it on fixed spheres. The motion of the planets was explained by the third-century AD astronomer, Ptolemy, by more complicated circular motions called epicycles. In Europe, this became the accepted description of the Universe. It was used by the Church alongside, and reinforcing, the Bible as part of the basis of its teaching.

Nevertheless by the sixteenth century, things were beginning to go wrong. Ptolemy's predictions for the positions of the Sun and Moon, vital for working out the calendar and the timing of Easter, were becoming increasingly inaccurate. Nicholas Copernicus published a theory in 1543 which put forward that the Sun was at the centre of the Universe with the Earth and planets revolving around it. Although this gave a more accurate calendar, it led to even more complications. Copernicus couldn't explain why people were not flung off the moving Earth and why the stars didn't seem to move relative to each other. As he expected, Copernicus was ridiculed by some of his fellow scientists. The astronomer Tycho Brahe offered a compromise system that had the Earth fixed at the centre of the Universe, with the planets orbiting the Sun, which in turn orbited the Earth.

Then Giordano Bruno, an heretical priest, took up Copernicus' theory along with other wild, magical ideas, insisting that it meant that the Earth was not the only inhabited world and that there must be many races on other planets which God was also interested in 'saving'. Bruno also incited Britain and France to oppose Spain and this led to his execution by burning by the Church in 1600.

Challenging the evidence

It is not known who invented the telescope, but by 1609 Galileo had made one and was using it for his astronomy.

Activity

Build a simple telescope and make some astronomical observations.

You will need: Two convex lenses, cardboard or a cardboard tube, sticky tape.

Hold the two lenses in a line with one lens close to your eye. Look through them at some distant object. Note the distance between the two lenses when you get a magnified image. Fix the lenses in a tube at this distance apart. Use your telescope to examine the Moon.

- Does the telescope make any details on the Moon clearer?
- What problems do you find with this simple telescope?

▲ **Galileo**

▲ **The Moon as seen through Galileo's telescope**

He soon discovered that the Moon had mountains, valleys and 'seas', that Jupiter had moons, that the Sun had spots, that Saturn had 'ears' (the rings) and that Venus had phases like the Moon. When Galileo published his observations, they were denounced by most of his fellow scientists, as he expected. The Jesuit mathematicians and Pope Paul V initially supported Galileo. However, when Galileo used his theory to question the literal truth of the Bible, some sections of the Church were furious. In 1616, Galileo was told by the Pope (and agreed) to stop discussing the Copernican theory as though it were established fact and to stress that it was just an hypothesis. Copernicus' book was suspended in 1614. In 1623, however, he wrote a fierce attack on a book about comets seen in 1618. Galileo's work was dedicated to the new Pope, Mafeo Barberini, but the powerful Jesuits who had written the book were very angry.

Galileo's friends and the new Pope urged Galileo to write a major book setting out clearly the claims of the rival theories of Aristotle/Ptolemy and Copernicus. He was also asked to include the Pope's own views (an attempt at a theological/scientific compromise). Galileo wrote the book as a dialogue between scholars but made a big mistake. He presented the Pope's views through a character called Simplicio - a much too obvious insult. The Pope's views were made to sound ridiculous and he was furious. Galileo was arrested and put on trial by the Inquisition.

The trial

Galileo's trial was a result of political manoeuvring rather than religious faith. With the growth in popularity of Martin Luther and the Protestants, the Catholic Church, and especially its more corrupt leaders, were under threat. The Protestants claimed that people should use the Bible as a guide rather than the Church's teaching. Only by taking an even more literal (fundamentalist) view of the Bible than the Protestants could the Catholic Church fight back. With the Pope turned against Galileo, and the apparent clash between Galileo's theories and the Bible, Galileo's enemies saw their chance to discredit his theories and maintain the Church's authority.

At the trial, Galileo pleaded that he had not intended to support the Copernican theory. At his age of 70, he knew that it was illegal to torture him, but the humiliation of his position made him agree to a swift public confession and sentence of house arrest. Galileo lived out the rest of his life quietly, writing important books on the motion of objects. Legend says that he persisted to mumble 'and yet it moves'.

Other scholars became afraid for their lives after Galileo's trial and scientific research almost ceased in Roman Catholic Europe. Copernicus' theories remained banned for 300 years. In Protestant Northern Europe, Galileo's ideas were accepted and people like Isaac Newton pushed further ahead in the exploration of the Universe. The Pope finally pardoned Galileo in the late 1980s.

GALILEO GALILEI
1564–1642

In the sixteenth century, Italy was the centre of learning in Europe. Galileo was born in Pisa and studied medicine there. He became interested in mathematics and physics and moved to the university at Padua in 1591. In 1610, the Medici family invited him to Florence to become court physician and mathematician, and this gave him the financial security he needed. When he was 35, Marina Gamba from Venice joined him and they had two daughters and a son but they were never married. Galileo was a proud man and considered himself a good Christian. His personal conviction was that truth came both from practical observations of nature and from the Bible.

Galileo performed many experiments. Some of these experiments resulted in his laws of motion and made him famous. He also wrote about how science should be done - he said that there were some things which could be measured and others which could not. He also said that a scientific problem should be examined by experiment and the results used to form a theory which should predict further results that can be tested. If the theory were proved there could be no disagreement.

▲ **Galileo's trial by the Inquisition**

Now try these

1. Galileo is often referred to as a 'martyr of science'. How true do you think this is?
2. Galileo's trial is sometimes seen as a battle between science and religion. Do you think this was how Galileo saw it?
3. Why do you think some Church leaders wanted Galileo silenced?
4. What was the effect of Galileo's trial on people's understanding of the Universe?

2.2 THE ORIGIN OF THE SPECIES

How did people, plants and animals come to be as they are? This question has been asked by people throughout history. The Creation story in Genesis, chapter 1 of the Bible, has provided the answer for Christians in the past and for some today. In 1859, Charles Darwin published *The Origin of Species*. This book offered a different answer and the Theory of Evolution was adopted by most scientists. How did Darwin arrive at his theory and how was it received by learned people?

Unchanged or evolving

The Genesis stories suggest a relatively young, unchanging world. The first suggestions that the world had evolved came in the seventeenth century.

Late in the eighteenth century, Lamarck came up with a recurring idea - the inheritance of acquired characteristics. Lamarck said that species were affected by their environment. For instance, giraffes gradually grew longer and longer necks by reaching up to the tops of trees and passing on this characteristic to their offspring.

George Cuvier, the early nineteenth-century French geologist, thought that catastrophes in the past had completely wiped out species which were no longer living, but could be found as fossils. He didn't think that surviving species had changed in any way but had just increased in number to fill the gaps.

In 1830, Charles Lyell began publication of his *Principles of Geology* which described the processes of erosion and sedimentation that slowly altered the appearance of the Earth. This evolution of land and sea obviously affected the creatures living on and in it. The books were eagerly read by Charles Darwin.

Charles Lyell saw no conflict between his ideas and his conviction that God had created the Earth and everything in it, and many Churchmen supported his ideas.

The voyage of the *Beagle*

For five years Darwin lived in the cramped quarters of the *Beagle* on its voyage of exploration around the world. During that time he collected thousands of biological and geological samples and filled notebooks with observations. He saw proof of Lyell's theory of the Earth's gradual evolution, but also witnessed catastrophic events such as an earthquake in Chile. He observed coral reefs and decided, correctly, that they were caused by subsidence of the sea floor. He noted that there were many examples of similar creatures existing in widely separated parts of the Earth

Activity

Darwin was very interested in the way that people have affected the evolution of domesticated animals. By *selective breeding* in animals (eg cow, sheep, dog), a huge variety of characteristics have been produced from a single species.

Examine, either in real life or in books, a number of varieties of a particular species of domesticated animal or plant. Make a list of the similarities and differences between each variety.

- What similarities are there between all the varieties of a particular species?
- What are the advantages (to animals or to humans) of the special characteristics of each variety?
- How have the different varieties been obtained?

CHARLES DARWIN
1809–82

Darwin was born in Shrewsbury. In 1825, he was sent to Edinburgh University to study medicine but did not like it. After two years, his father sent him to Cambridge University to study divinity to prepare for a career as a clergyman. Although a Christian all his life, Darwin was more interested in natural history and geology than divinity. As a result of friendships with well-known scientists he was offered the position of naturalist on the *Beagle*. Despite his father's disapproval, he left for the five-year voyage in 1831. In 1838, he married his cousin, Emma, and settled in Kent. For the remainder of his life he suffered from ill-health and rarely left home. It is possible that he picked up a disease in South America.

▲ **HMS *Beagle*, Darwin's home for five years**

(eg ostriches in South Africa and rheas in South America), while creatures in Australia seemed to have a different Creator. But most important, he noted the slight differences between varieties of creatures that obviously had a common ancestor, such as the finches of the Galapagos Islands which had beaks suited to their different sources of food on each island.

▲ **Darwin's drawings of finches from the Galapagos Islands, showing differences in the beaks**

Back in London in 1836, Darwin first had to catalogue all his samples. For this he had the help of Richard Owen, a greatly respected palaeontologist and founder of the London Natural History Museum. Gradually, Darwin came to the conclusion that species did change and late in 1838 he realised that the changes were the result of variation in the offspring of sexual reproduction and the competition for a limited supply of food. Only those offspring best suited to the environment would survive and reproduce.

Darwin's ideas developed over the years but he was reluctant to publish them as he knew they were controversial. However in 1856, Alfred Wallace, a young biologist sent him a letter describing a theory very similar to his own. Darwin was urged to publish his ideas jointly with Wallace, which they did. In 1859 Darwin finally marshalled all his facts and evidence to publish *On the Origin of Species*. It was a bestseller and many scientists immediately realised its significance. It only mentioned humans briefly but Darwin published *The Descent of Man* in 1871.

Now try these

1 In what ways does Darwin's Theory of Natural Selection differ from Lamarck's theory of acquired characteristics?

2 Why did Darwin attach a lot of importance to the selective breeding of domestic animals?

3 Why were certain sectors of the Christian Church anxious to disprove Darwin's theory?

4 Some people have described the Oxford debate as a victory for science over religion. Is this a fair comment? Explain your answer.

5 How is it possible to believe in both evolution and God's creation?

▲ **How cartoonists saw Darwin in 1871**

The great debate

Darwin's theory had its enemies, ranging from some Christians who saw it as leaving little room for God in the processes of Creation, to some atheists who saw its determinism as leaving too much room for a creating God. Darwin's greatest opponent turned out to be his former friend, Richard Owen. Darwin gained a champion in Thomas Huxley, a young zoologist and a brilliant speaker. In 1860, the British Association for the Advancement of Science held its annual meeting in Oxford. A debate was arranged between Huxley and Bishop Wilberforce, a believer in the literal truth of the Creation. Owen helped the Bishop who was not a scientist, but in the debate he made a number of errors in his ridicule of Darwin's theory. He ended by asking Huxley if 'it was through his grandfather or grandmother that he claimed descent from a monkey'. Huxley replied that 'he preferred an ape for an ancestor to a man who introduced ridicule into a scientific debate'. As a result of this famous debate, many more people became interested in Darwin's theory.

Fundamentalist Christian churches have continued to insist on the truth of the Creation story. Court cases in the USA and Australia up to the present day, have forced the teaching of Creationism in school science lessons along with or instead of evolution theories.

2.3 JUNGLES IN ANTARCTICA

'God said, "Let the waters under heaven be gathered into one place so that dry land may appear"; and so it was. God called the dry land earth, and the gathering of the waters he called seas.'
(*The Bible*, Genesis, chapter 1, verses 9–10)

Travel around the world and you will see massive mountains, deep canyons, oceans as deep as the mountains are high. These features of the Earth seem unchanging and yet people have always looked for reasons for why the Earth appears as it does. For hundreds of years, Christians and Jews looked to the Genesis story in the Bible for an answer, while followers of other religions had their own tales.

What is the truth? What evidence is there? How have new techniques altered our theories of how the Earth has become how it is?

Activity

Models of the Earth

A You will need: A balloon, paste (or Pritt stick), flour or talc, string. Blow up the balloon until it is firm and then tie a piece of string around the end of it. Cover the balloon with paste and while it is still damp, sprinkle flour or talc over it. Allow the paste to dry. Carefully release the string so that the balloon deflates slightly. Watch what happens to the coating.

B You will need: A large beaker, tripod and gauze, Bunsen burner, flour or talc. Fill the beaker with cold water and place it on the tripod. When the water has settled, lightly sprinkle it with the flour or talc. Warm the water in the beaker slowly. Watch what happens to the flour on the surface.

1 Describe what you see in both experiments.

2 Both experiments are **models** of what might have happened to the surface of the Earth. Use your observations to think up two different theories for the formation of continents and mountain ranges.

4004 and all that

The story of the Creation in the Bible suggests that the Earth has remained largely the same since God created it. In the 1650s, Archbishop James Ussher added up the ages of all the people in the Bible and came to the conclusion that Creation must have taken place in 4004 BC. This left very little time for geological processes to alter the shape of the continents. This problem was recognised by scientists such as Edmund Halley in 1715 who thought the Earth must be older.

Abraham Werner believed that the Earth had been initially covered by ocean and that over a period of a million years,

▲ **The bibical image of Creation**

Myths and legends

Some of the ideas of early civilisations seem fanciful now but were real to the people of the time. Many peoples, such as the ancient inhabitants of Mesopotamia (now Iraq) saw the Earth as a flat disc covered by a dome of the heavens. To the Egyptians, the dome was represented by the goddess, Nut, supported by the air god Shu, with the Earth represented by the god Qeb lying on his side. The Mayans, in present-day Mexico, believed that their land was the back of a lizard lying in a vast ocean. Certainly motions of the lizard would explain the frequent earthquakes. The Chinese were the first to take a more scientific look at the Earth and as early as the first BC, they realised that fossils were the remains of dead animals and plants.

ABRAHAM WERNER
1749–1817

Abraham was born in a mining area of Germany. He was taught mining techniques and studied at Leipzig University. He returned to his home in Freiburg as a lecturer. He was interested in the geology of his area and his research gave him the idea that rocks were mostly layers formed in the original ocean described in the Bible.

bits of sediment had settled to the bottom of the ocean. This deposition slowly built up the continents, aided by volcanoes and earthquakes.

Another idea was that the Earth was originally a molten ball that was slowly cooling. In 1830, Elie de Beaumont suggested that as the Earth cooled it contracted. This would mean that the crust would crack and crumple, hence producing mountain ranges.

In 1912, Alfred Wegener suggested that the continents drifted over the Earth's surface, splitting and colliding with each other. In 1928, Arthur Holmes suggested that this movement could be caused by convection currents in the molten mantle beneath the Earth's crust.

Which theory was right? Where was the evidence?

Radioactive fossils and magnetic rocks

As early as the 1670s it was observed that rock strata were often folded and that fossils of sea creatures could often be found in rocks high above the sea level. This, suggested Nils Stenson, meant that rocks were once under the sea.

In the 1920s, Holmes used the presence of radioactive elements in rocks to work out the age of the rocks and fossils. This work proved Wegener's ideas that rocks from places as far apart as South America and Africa were identical in age and composition.

Another new technique - measuring the magnetism in rocks on the seabed - brought forward more evidence. Research was carried out by the HMS *Challenger* expedition in the 1950s. It was found that a pattern of magnetism was common to rocks on both sides of the mid-ocean ridges. This could only mean that the rocks were forming and spreading out from the ridges. In the 1970s, the Glomar *Challenger* carried out a series of drillings that confirmed the theory that the continents move. Fossils were found in Antarctica that showed that the frozen continent once had a tropical climate and hence must have been nearer the Equator.

Proof and acceptance?

It took 50 years for Wegener's theory, now known as **plate tectonics**, to be accepted. For many years, American and European scientists ignored his ideas. One reason may have been because as a German he wasn't very popular after World War I. However, its unpopularity was largely because the evidence later provided by the two *Challenger* missions was not available. Now that plate tectonics is accepted, it is proving helpful in predicting where mineral resources may be found - and creating problems. Since the Antarctic has not always been a frozen desert it harbours vast resources of coal, oil and minerals that countries would like to exploit. There is now a great risk that this unique and fragile environment will be damaged.

ALFRED WEGENER
1880–1930

Wegener was educated at Heidelburg, Innsbruck and Berlin. He was a doctor of astronomy but eventually became a meteorologist. He was interested in the past climate of the Earth and became interested by the presence of fossils of creatures from different climates in the same areas. He decided that there had once been only one continent, **Pangaea**, that had broken up and the remains had drifted around the Earth to their present positions. However, he had no idea how this had happened. He died on his fourth expedition to Greenland.

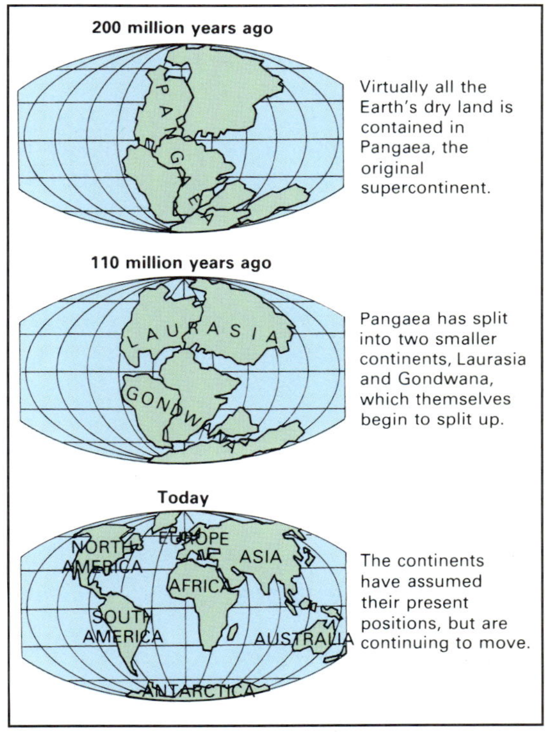

▲ **Wegener's map showing the continents originally joined together as Pangaea**

Now try these

1 How did the changing ideas about the Earth agree or disagree with stories in the Bible? Do you think this might have affected people's religious beliefs?

2 Explain the formation of the Antarctic continent using **a** de Beaumont's theory of the shrinking Earth and **b** Wegener's theory of continental drift.

3 Discuss whether the resources of the Antarctic should be used or protected.

2.4 LEGACY OF ALEXANDER

If you look at a list of Nobel Prize winners, the names are mainly European. It is easy to make the mistake that science is something that developed in Europe over the last few hundred years. In fact, even modern science owes a lot to the philosophers and craftsmen of Ancient Greece, Egypt, India and Arabia all drawn together in the city of Alexandria.

An Ancient Egyptian dye recipe

'Crush and mix with water two parts of krimnos *and three parts of dyer's alum. Put the wool in and it will be scarlet red. If it is to be leek green, add powdered sulphur with water. If it is to be quince yellow, add soda and water.'*

Dyer's alum is potassium aluminium sulphate ($KAl[SO_4]_2$) and soda is sodium carbonate decahydrate ($Na_2CO_3.10H_2O$). Apart from being a red dye, we do not know what *krimnos* is, but red cabbage or beetroot seems to work well. How successful is the recipe?

You will need: Wool (preferably undyed), alum, soda, sulphur, red cabbage and/or beetroot, beakers, stirring rods, tripod and gauze, Bunsen burner. The dye mixture will probably need heating.

- Is the dye colourfast or does it wash off easily?

Alchemy – the secret art!

The ancient Egyptians left behind rolls of papyrus that explain how to make metal alloys for jewellery, coloured dyes for cloth and imitation gems using cheap stones. The apparatus and methods that these craftsmen used were copied by the scholars of Alexandria in the quest for the **Philosopher's stone** which would turn lead into gold. This was not such a ridiculous idea as it may now appear because it was once thought that all metals were mixtures of the four elements - earth, air, fire and water.

The early alchemists developed many of the techniques used in modern chemistry for reacting and separating substances. The most important period for alchemy in Alexandria was from 200 to 300 AD. During this time, **distillation** was developed for collecting liquids such as alcohol. The alchemists were influenced by the old religions of Persia and India, as well as the new Christianity. They used complex language to hide their knowledge and made use of symbols such as the planets, the Sun and the Moon for each of the metals. Strange and mythical creatures like the salamander and phoenix represented fire.

ALEXANDER THE GREAT
356BC–323BC

Alexander became King of Greece and Macedonia in 338 BC and almost immediately set out on a war of conquest that took him to Egypt, Persia and India. When he died in 323 BC his empire split up but Greek philosophy, trade and culture had been spread across the Middle East. Alexander's influence had its most lasting effect in Egypt under Alexander's general, Ptolemy Soter, who founded the city of Alexandria with its museum and library. The museum became the first state-supported university and research centre. Philosophers came from all over the Middle East to study the hundreds of thousands of manuscripts stored in the library. Alexandria remained a centre of learning after Rome took over Egypt but its reputation faded in the fourth and fifth centuries AD. Scholars fled with some of the books when the library came under threat from invaders and mobs. The Christian Church thought that some of the scholars were heretics. The end of Alexandria finally came in 640 AD when followers of Islam invaded Egypt.

▲ **An alembic - an early distillation equipment**

- What properties of metals such as tin, lead and silver suggest that they are all just different mixtures of the four elements?
- Why was distillation a useful technique for alchemists to learn?

Toys and stars

The Ancient Greeks have a reputation for thinking about problems, but it was the Alexandrian scholars who began to carry out practical scientific experiments. Astronomy was a popular study. Eratosthenes, the chief librarian in Alexandria in 235 BC, calculated the circumference of the Earth by measuring the lengths of shadows at various points on the Earth's surface. Hipparchos made careful measurements during an eclipse of the Sun to calculate the distance from the Earth to the Sun and Moon. Hipparchos' observations of the planets were used by the astronomer Ptolemy in his theory concerning the motion of the Sun and planets around the Earth. Other ideas were forgotten - in about 250 BC Aristarchos suggested that the Earth orbited the Sun but he had no proof.

Other scholars were more down-to-earth and applied their ideas to inventing machines, and although most seem to be toys, some have wider use. Archimedes developed a screw that could lift water. This is still in use in Middle Eastern countries. He also invented pulley systems that could greatly magnify the force applied by the operator. Around 60 AD, Hero carried out much research into air pressure (pneumatics) and light but only applied his discoveries to entertaining demonstrations, such as illusions with mirrors and his 'steam engine'.

Arabic science

When the Roman Empire collapsed in the fifth century, communities became cut off. The small, struggling communities that were left had little time to devote to science and the Alexandrian knowledge was lost. However, in Arabia the new religion of Islam was expanding. The conquerors moved across North Africa and the Middle East to India. The culture and knowledge that they found in these countries was adopted and Arabian scholars collected Greek and Alexandrian books. Jabir ibn Hayyan developed the ideas of the Alexandrian alchemist, Zosimus. He said that all metals were mixtures of mercury and sulphur. Thabat ibn Qurra translated Archimedes' works and ibn al-Haytham examined Alexandrian writings on light and introduced the idea that the ray of light emitted from a light source was reflected off polished surfaces. Al-Khwarizmi adopted the Indian idea of using the numerals 1 to 9.

During the wars between Christian Europe and Islamic Arabia in the Middle Ages, Arabic books began to reach European scholars. The Europeans rediscovered Greek and Alexandrian science and used the Arabic science for the basis of their own research.

ARCHIMEDES
287–212 BC

Archimedes was born in Sicily and returned there from Alexandria to help his relative, King Hieron, fight off the Romans. In Alexandria he learnt to carry out experiments to test theories which he expressed mathematically. While trying to solve the problem of Hieron's crown (Was it pure gold or an alloy with silver?) he discovered the principle that bears his name - an object displaces its own volume of water when submerged. He was also a mathematician, finding an accurate value of π and working out the area of curved objects. He was killed by one of the Roman invaders of Sicily.

▲ **The Archimedes screw - used to raise water**

Now try these

1. Very few Alexandrian inventions were made use of. Why do you think the Egyptian people had little use for complicated machinery?
2. Why were so many scholars attracted to Alexandria?
3. How does a pulley system magnify forces? Draw a diagram of a pulley system to help you explain.
4. 'The growth of science in Medieval Europe was largely due to the Crusades.' Discuss whether this statement is justified.

2.5 CHINESE INVENTION, EUROPEAN PROGRESS

Today, as always, China remains a mysterious place with a language, society and culture that we barely understand. The thousands of years of Chinese history are still unknown to us. Yet many things that we take for granted in Europe and America have come to us from China. The progress in science and technology that has been made in Europe in the last 500 years has often been a result of Chinese science that took place up to 1500 years earlier.

Dynasty

China covers an area the size of Europe and yet for most of the last 2000 years it has been under the control of a single government. In the west there are vast mountain ranges that cut it off from India and the Middle East. To the north there are the barren steppes of Russia, once the home of nomadic tribes. To the south and east, the land is flatter and crossed by the two main rivers, the Yellow River and the Yangtze with their many tributaries. These rivers bring silt from the mountains and fertilise the plains. The Chinese were hence able to feed a huge population from the earliest times.

While the Egyptians were building the pyramids, a similar Bronze Age civilisation dominated by feudal lords was developing in China. By 200 BC all of China had been united, initially under the short-lived Chhin dynasty, and then the Han dynasty which lasted 400 years. Invasion from the north and civil war caused changes of government and at times the empire was split in two or three parts. In the tenth century AD, however, there came the final unification which has lasted to the present day.

Activity

Making a compass

You will need: A magnet, an iron needle, card, cotton, cork, a dish.

Magnetise the needle by stroking it repeatedly in one direction with one pole of your magnet. Hold the magnet well away from the needle in between strokes. When your needle magnet is strong enough to pick up some iron filings you can build your compass. The needle must be allowed to swing freely and you will need to mark out the compass points.

- Why was the compass of great use to early navigators?

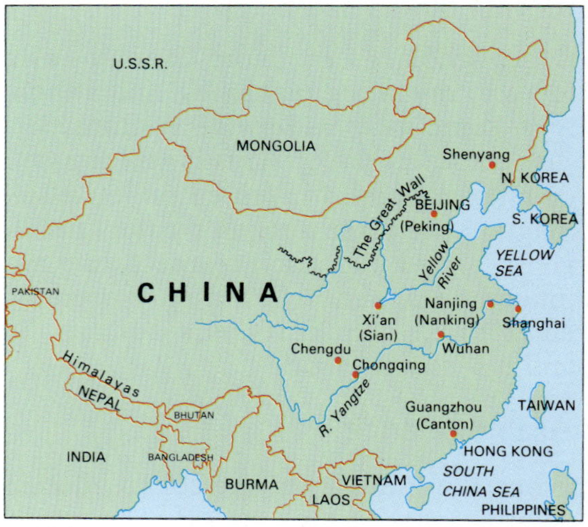

▲ China

A comparison of the times

Date	China	Rest of the World
BC		
2600	The Yangshao feudal civilisation	Egypt: pyramids built
200	The Chhin and Han dynasties unify China	Rome takes control of the Mediterranean
AD		
221	Han dynasty ends: Empire divided in three parts	Roman Empire at its greatest extent
581	Re-united under the Sui dynasty	Roman Empire fallen; Europe in 'Dark Ages'
650	Thang dynasty; Grand Canal built	Moslem expansion in Arabia and North Africa
906	Empire split	Anglo-Saxon Britain becomes Christian
1127	Re-united under Sung dynasty	Normans control Britain; universities are established in Europe
1368	Ming dynasty	Renaissance and voyages of discovery
1644	Chhing dynasty	English Civil War
1912	Emperor deposed	World War I about to start (1914)
1949	Communist People's Republic formed	1945 End of World War II

Running such a huge country has required a highly organised government. The Han dynasty invented the civil service which managed each village in the name of the Emperor. Entry to the civil service was by examination. Each year hopeful students would study hard for the oral exams and, if successful, were sure of a well-paid career. The Emperor controlled all trade. In Europe, merchants grew rich by encouraging the trade in new goods. China, however, never developed a powerful class of traders.

Science and technology

The rivers of China were the source of the Emperor's power. They ensured successful harvests and a means of transporting food to central depots so that the Emperor could control the prices. But in the wet season the rivers flooded and caused tremendous damage. In the Han dynasty, massive engineering works were undertaken to control the flow of water and the rivers were turned into canals. In the sixth century an additional waterway, the Grand Canal, was dug to link the Yellow and Yangtze rivers. Five and a half million workers supervised by 50 000 police were employed on the project. The canal is still the main means of transport between north and south China.

▲ The Grand Canal – still in use after 1500 years

The engineers who designed the canal were part of the civil service. Other scientists were also employed by the Emperor to solve other problems. Machines were invented to move water and aid farmers. New strains of rice were developed to increase yields. Deep drilling was invented to reach salt buried deep underground. Astronomers watched the skies to maintain a calendar and to observe signs that they believed foretold the future. Chinese astronomers recorded events that Europeans ignored, such as the supernova in 1006 that has produced the Crab Nebula seen today.

Earthquakes often occur in parts of China. In the seventh century, Chang Heng invented an instrument that could detect an earthquake occurring hundreds of miles away and indicate its direction. When it produced its first results that an earthquake had happened, watchers didn't believe it as they had felt nothing. However, days later messengers reported that an earthquake had indeed occurred.

Contact

Despite being isolated, China was not totally without contact with the rest of the world. Even during the Han dynasty there were contacts with the Roman Empire in Syria. In the eighth century the Chinese Empire spread westwards and re-established trade along the Silk Road which took Chinese goods across the mountains, into Afghanistan and Iran, and on to Europe.

It was along the Silk Road that Marco Polo travelled in the thirteenth century. He stayed in China for years, before returning with wonderful tales which encouraged other traders to follow in his footsteps. This slender contact provided Europe with hints of Chinese science that led to great steps being made in science and technology. By the seventeenth century, Europeans were colonising all parts of the world. In 1644, the Ming dynasty was replaced by the Chhing, and Chinese scientists began to adopt the knowledge of European Christians, leaving behind their own philosophies.

Now try these

1 Why do you think that China remained under one government for so long while Europe split into many nations?

2 Why was a seismograph for detecting earthquakes of use to the government?

3 Science has developed rapidly in Europe in the last 500 years. Why didn't similar progress occur in China?

▲ The Emperor's seismograph – a hanging weight inside knocks a ball out of one of the dragon's mouths into the mouth of the frog below if an earth tremor occurs

2.5 CHINESE INVENTION, EUROPEAN PROGRESS

Oriental discoveries

Pointing south

The magnetic mineral, lodestone, is found all over the world and early civilisations were intrigued by its magical properties. The Chinese constantly looked for signs to guide them and they used boards with prophetic markings to help them make decisions. In the third century BC, some diviners started using pieces of lodestone on the board. Soon, spoons made of lodestone were being spun in the middle of the board to point out decisions. The fortune tellers recognised that the spoon always pointed in the same direction - to the south. By the first century AD, the spoons were mounted on needles or floated in water to reduce friction and 500 years later it was discovered that iron needles could be magnetised by stroking with a lodestone. These compasses were used to lay out buildings and public projects and by the tenth century were also being used by Chinese sailors. The use of the magnetic compass filtered westwards and was first used by European sailors a hundred years later. Without the compass, the voyages of discovery undertaken by Portuguese, Spanish and British sailors in the fifteenth and sixteenth centuries would have been impossible. However, the Chinese made little use of their invention and were uninterested in probing the properties of magnets.

Recording bureaucracy

Early writing was done on clay tablets, papyrus and parchment which are difficult to make and expensive: as a result, there are few books and written records. In China, however, the bureaucracy set up by the Han dynasty in 200 BC to control the vast empire demanded complete records, and many messages were carried across the country. This demand for writing materials stimulated the development of paper around 0 AD. Paper can be made in large quantities from old cloth such as linen, and cotton and plant material such as straw. The cloth is pounded into a pulp with water, and then stirred in vats before pouring over gauze trays to form sheets of paper. Paper was relatively cheap and could keep the armies of Chinese civil servants supplied. In the ninth century, the Chinese also began using wooden blocks to print onto paper.

In the eighth century, during the wars between China and the Muslims, a few Chinese paper-makers were captured in Samarkand by the Arabs. The Arab world quickly recognised the importance of paper but it was another five centuries before Western Europe gained paper-making knowledge. However, it was in Spain that mills were invented to beat the pulp. In Germany, moveable type was invented by Johannes Gutenberg in the fifteenth century. This made books much cheaper and simpler to print.

- How do you think knowledge of the compass reached Europe from China?
- How did sailors navigate at sea before compasses had been invented?

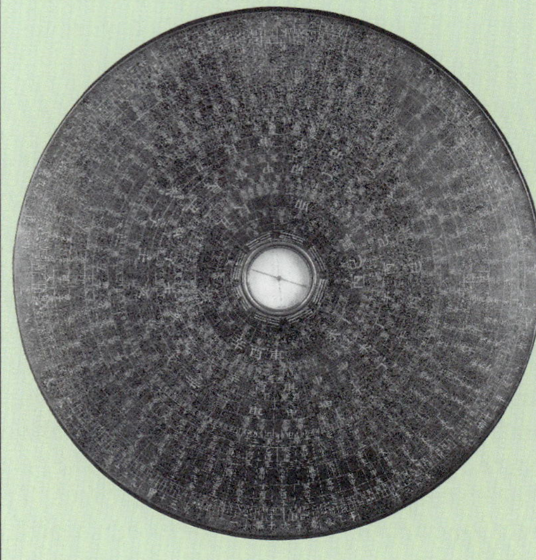

▲ **A compass was part of the geomancer's prediction device**

- Few examples of early Chinese books remain. Why do you think this is?
- European languages made the printing of books with moveable type a straightforward process. Why wasn't this possible in China?

▲ **An ancient Chinese printed book**

Making a bang

Chinese chemists have contributed much to our knowledge of substances. The Chinese chemists worked for the Emperor producing dyes such as Imperial Yellow for cloth, and inks for the writing of records. The chemists followed Taoism which sought physical immortality. This stimulated chemists to develop substances that would preserve bodies for thousands of years. Recently, the body of a woman who died in 186 BC was discovered in a state resembling a body dead for only a week.

In the eighth century, Chinese chemists found a mixture of sulphur, charcoal and saltpetre that burnt fiercely and would explode in containers - gunpowder! It had its first military use in the wars with the invading Tartars who eventually formed the Chin dynasty in 1115. Chinese armies used gunpowder in grenades, bombs and rockets. Like other inventions, the knowledge of gunpowder slowly penetrated to the west, but here it was used in a different way - in cannons. The Moors in Spain used gunpowder around 1250 to fire stones from a simple bucket-shaped mortar and by the middle of the fourteenth century, bronze and cast iron cannon were in use all over Europe.

- Once the knowledge reached Europe the use of gunpowder spread quickly. Why was this?
- What other technology did the manufacture of firearms and cannon require?

▲ **Gunpowder is used in these spectacular Chinese fireworks**

Healing pins

Two important Chinese beliefs were, first, that there was a close link between humans (the microcosm) and the Universe (the macrocosm), and second that there is a 'vital spirit' or air that flowed around the body. Both these ideas were part of the theory of acupuncture which was developed before 600 BC.

Acupuncture was used for the healing of all types of disease as well as for stopping pain. Needles are inserted into the skin at points corresponding to compass points, patterns of stars and the lines of flow of the vital spirit. The theory of the flow of the spirit led Chinese doctors to investigate the blood. The circulation of the blood was discovered during the Han dynasty, 1600 years before Harvey made the same discovery in Europe. Medicine, like other professions, was highly organised in China. By the fifth century there were medical schools for training doctors and state-run hospitals.

In recent years, acupuncture has become accepted by western doctors particularly as an anaesthetic.

The Chinese made many other discoveries and inventions. Mechanical clocks were invented to help astronomers measure the motion of the stars. Chinese porcelain was sought after for centuries until western potters managed to imitate it. But out of all these inventions, few became widely used by the people who followed in the footsteps of these early Chinese scientists.

- Why do you think that western scientists found it difficult to accept acupuncture?
- What reasons can you think of to explain the long gap between the Chinese and European discoveries of the circulation of the blood?

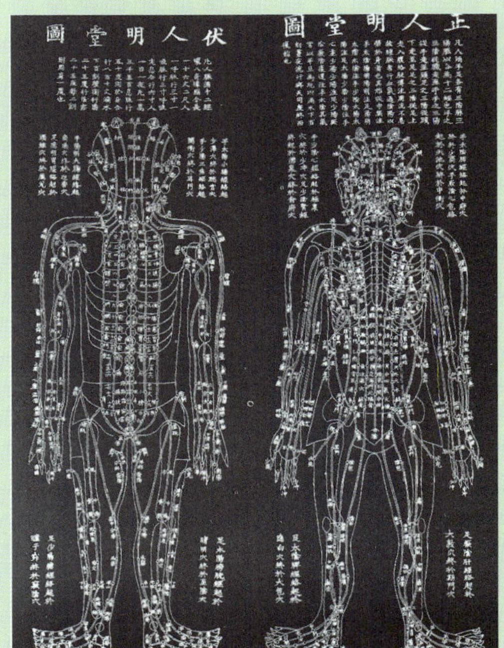

▲ **A plan of the acupuncture points and flow lines of the vital spirit**

2.6 WOMEN IN SCIENCE

■ How many famous women composers, artists, architects or scientists can you think of?

It is likely that your list will be fairly short. This doesn't prove that women are not creative or scientific, but is merely a result of the low esteem that society has held women in until now. Some will say that this state of affairs still exists. For thousands of years, women were treated as inferior to men and it was the men who had the power and wealth. This was as true of the civilisations of China and Japan as it was of Europe and Africa. In Britain until quite recently a married woman had no possessions of her own and was effectively owned by her husband. Women were needed to work - on the land, down mines and in factories - but education was denied to them so there was no chance of self-improvement.

Some women nevertheless made contributions to science. Caroline Herschel made almost as many astronomical discoveries as her brother William but she was not invited to meetings of the Royal Society and unlike her brother she was not rewarded with an official position in the court of King George III.

The situation began to improve during the nineteenth century when schools for girls opened and started to offer subjects other than basic reading, writing and needlework. However, women were still denied places at universities.

The position was a little easier in Europe where Marie Curie became the first female professor at the University of Paris. However, this post was offered to her only after the death of her husband Pierre and the award of a Nobel prize to them both for the discovery of radium (see *What is Science?*, p. 14).

Women gained more freedom after World Wars I and II, but it has still been difficult for them to maintain their careers while bringing up children. Government and society still see the man as the main earner and master of the house, even though in practice this often is not the case. Thus until now a woman has had to be extremely determined to achieve success and has usually had to be **better** than her male rivals in order to overcome male prejudice.

Today, educational opportunities in Britain are open to women as much as to men. Women are welcomed in industry as engineers as well as scientists. WISE (women into science and engineering), for example, promotes careers in science and engineering for women. Nevertheless, there are still very few well-known women in science. Perhaps learning about a few that have made it will encourage young women of today to beome the scientists, engineers and industrialists of tomorrow.

▲ **Women provided cheap labour for factory and mine owners**

Activity

■ What part do women play in science and industry today?

Look through newspapers and magazines for mention of women in science and industry. Try magazines such as *New Scientist*, *Scientific American*, *Omni*, *The Economist*, computing magazines, etc. Make notes on each woman that you find.

■ Do women's names appear in articles about one branch of science more than they do others?

WISE promotes science education for women ▶

Role models

DOROTHY MARY CROWFOOT HODGKIN
born 1910

Dorothy spent her childhood in Africa with her parents and was very interested in the archaeological sites that her father looked after. However, she decided to study chemistry at Oxford University. She then went to Cambridge University to continue studies on X-ray crystallography. She returned to Oxford in 1934 to begin her research into the structure of large molecules such as penicillin, vitamin B_{12} and insulin. Dorothy married in 1937. X-ray crystallography had only just been developed and in its early years needed careful experimentation, an immense number of mathematical calculations, and imagination to see the correct structure from all the figures. In the 1960s, computers made the work simpler. In 1964, Dorothy became the third woman to win the Nobel Prize for Chemistry.

▲ Dorothy Hodgkin

MARIA GOEPPERT MAYER
1906–72

Maria was born in Germany and took up physics after studying maths at Göttingen University. In 1930, she married an American chemist, Joseph Mayer, and they moved to John Hopkins University in the USA. She was studying the properties of elements heavier than uranium but found it difficult to find somewhere that would employ a woman. When World War II started, her work became part of the atomic bomb project and at last she had people working for her. Her work on uranium hexafluoride contributed to the process for separating uranium-235 for bombs and nuclear reactors. After the war, Maria worked on the structure of the atomic nucleus at Chicago and won the Nobel Prize for Physics in 1963.

RITA LEVI-MONTALCINI
born 1909

Rita had to overcome the difficulties of being a Jew in fascist Italy in the 1930s and the disapproval of her parents when she entered medical school. She qualified as a doctor just as World War II began and she then had to go into hiding. She married G. Levi and started research on growth of nerves in chicken embryos. After the war she worked at Washington University and discovered the substance responsible for the growth of nerves. She returned to Rome to be Director of the Laboratory for Cell Biology until her retirement in 1979. She was awarded the Nobel Prize for Medicine in 1986.

SUSAN JOCELYN BELL
born 1943

Jocelyn made her most famous discovery in 1967 while still a research student at Cambridge University. She was investigating radio waves in space using a radio telescope. A source was producing a burst of radio waves at intervals of just over a second. She soon found that the radio bursts came from particular stars which were subsequently named **pulsars** (now known to be rotating neutron stars).

MARY LEAKEY
born 1913

Mary did not have a formal education but travelled with her father, a landscape painter, during her youth. She did attend some lectures on archaeology at University College, London. She worked at archaeological digs in England between 1930 and 1933 and joined Louis Leakey on an expedition to Olduvai Gorge in East Africa in 1935. They were married soon after. She has spent most of her life searching for remains of human ancestors, the **hominids**. In 1976, she led an expedition to Tanzania that found the earliest evidence of our ancestors – two sets of footprints 3.75 million years old.

Now try these

1. How would you encourage girls to study science?
2. Describe how you think one of the women above felt when she made her discovery.
3. How has life today made it easier (or harder) for girls to follow careers in science?

3.1 WHOSE EARTH?

The 1990s have been called 'the caring '90s' by some politicians. They mean that during the decade we shall care for the environment to preserve the Earth as a place to live. It seems that there are many problems to cope with - acid rain, ozone depletion, the greenhouse effect and toxic wastes, to name just a few. Some people blame these problems on scientists. It is even said that we shouldn't listen to scientists now when they offer ideas and solutions because science can't be trusted to help the environment. (Further details of these environmental concerns can be found in *Waste and pollution*, *Metals* and *The environment*.)

- Do you think scientists are responsible for our environmental problems? If it is not just scientists, who else is responsible?

▲ **Why are these trees dying?**

The mystery of the dying forests

During the 1970s people in Scandinavia and Germany became worried that a lot of trees in their forests were dying. They also noticed that fish were disappearing from lakes although the water appeared clear and clean. By the mid-1980s, many lakes in Norway and Sweden were empty of fish.

The mystery for scientists was rather like that facing doctors when they have a patient who feels unwell. The patient can describe the symptoms but the doctor has to sort through all the diseases that could produce those symptoms, then carry out tests before making a diagnosis.

Scientists had various theories for the death of the forests. They looked for evidence in tree samples, they carried out experiments on plants in laboratories and they compared forests in different parts of the world. Some of the theories that were tested were:

- a disease was attacking the trees (similar to the fungus that caused the Dutch Elm disease that destroyed thousands of elm trees in Britain)
- the trees were suffering from a lack of essential minerals (eg magnesium) that had been removed from the soil over a period of hundreds of years
- the trees were being damaged by acidic water.

- What problems do you think scientists had in testing these theories?

There were many uncertainties as scientists found evidence for one theory or another, but gradually it became accepted by most scientists that acidic water was the cause, particularly as it had been found that the dead lakes were also extremely acidic. What was more conclusive was that the rain in these areas was also often highly acidic (as low

Activity

How does acid affect plants?

We can't experiment on a forest but you can investigate the effect of acid on a smaller, faster-growing plant - cress.

Plan an investigation on the effects of acid on cress. You must decide which acids to use and ensure that it is a fair test.

You will need: Petri dishes, cress seeds, cotton wool, measuring cylinders, droppers, various acids.

- Do you think the cress should germinate before treating it with acid?

▲ **Didcot power station in Oxfordshire - a coal-fired power station**

as pH 1 or 2). However, acidity couldn't be the whole story as the symptoms did not exactly match the known effects of acids on plants. More work by scientists finally uncovered the fact that the acid water was dissolving metal compounds in the soil that were usually insoluble. Some of the dissolved metals, such as aluminium, were toxic to plants.

Despite the growing evidence, some scientists, particularly those working for the Central Electricity Generating Board (CEGB) in Britain preferred other theories. Even in the late 1980s, some scientists clung to the theory that trees were lacking certain nutrients.

■ Why do you think the CEGB was doing research on the forest and lake problem?

The source of the acid was the root of the problem. The main acid was found to be sulphuric acid, but nitric acid was also present. Both these acids are produced naturally, by volcanoes and thunderstorms. However, the Scandinavians and Germans noted that rainclouds passed over highly populated industrial areas before dropping rain on their forests and lakes. In these areas, power stations burnt coal and oil that contained sulphur, and motor vehicles produced nitrogen oxides in their exhausts. During the twentieth century, the amount of sulphur dioxide released into the atmosphere has increased a great deal. Political pressures have now built up to do something about the problem.

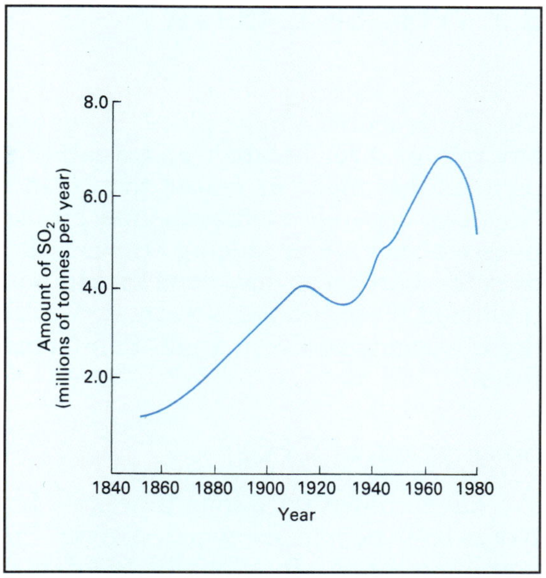

▲ **Changes in the production of sulphur dioxide by human activities since 1850**

The cure

Sulphur dioxide can be removed from the fumes of a power station by reacting the emissions with limestone. Germany has started a programme to convert all its power stations so that emissions of sulphur dioxide will be reduced. This process requires a lot of limestone which means more quarries and a large amount of solid waste, apart from being expensive. Britain has decided to import sulphur-free coal rather than spend a lot of money on converting all its power stations.

Scientists have discovered a compound of manganese that will convert the sulphur dioxide directly into sulphuric acid. The sulphuric acid would then be a valuable by-product for power stations. However, this method would be expensive and the scientists won't complete their trials for a number of years.

■ What do you think should be done to stop 'acid rain'?

Scientists are still investigating acid rain. They are finding out how the acid rain changes soil and looking for other ways to burn coal. Although liming lakes neutralises the acid, it is only partially successful and other cures are being considered.

Now try these

1 Plan a short TV debate on the dying forests. One side should support the 'shortage of magnesium' theory and the other, the 'acid rain' theory. Assume that both causes produce the same effects (ie yellowing leaves which fall from trees, leaving bare branches).

2 Motor vehicles are a major cause of acid rain. What suggestions can you make for reducing this problem?

3 Do you think scientists have done all that they can to solve the acid rain problem? If not, what else could they do?

Lakes have been limed to counteract the effects of the acid ▶

3.1 WHOSE EARTH?

The Earth seems a huge place. However, we can travel to any part of it for holidays and weather satellites give us pictures that make us realise that it isn't so big after all. Now two separate environmental problems caused by the lives we lead are producing effects that could affect life all over the Earth and may even end it. Some scientists predicted these problems years ago, while others denied there was any problem at all. Politicians preferred not to listen.

Sixty years of CFCs

We have known for a long time how important ozone is. Nowadays, people are worried about the ozone above cities and, more important globally, the damage done to the ozone layer in the upper atmosphere by chloro-fluoro-carbons (CFCs).

In 1930, Thomas Midgley suggested that dichloro,difluoro methane (CF_2Cl_2), also known as Freon12, would be a suitable fluid for refrigerators. It has a low boiling point, is non-flammable and non-toxic. Soon, similar compounds were being used in refrigerators, air-conditioning systems and fire extinguishers. In the 1960s, the same compounds began to be used in aerosols as the propellant (this gas provides the pressure by which the liquids are sprayed out). Finally, the same CFCs were used to 'blow' the foam used for packaging materials. In the 1970s and 1980s the use of CFCs rocketted.

But nobody had questioned what happened to the CFCs when they were released into the atmosphere. The gases are very unreactive and so remain in the air for a very long time. In 1971, Jim Lovelock discovered that CFCs were reaching the upper atmosphere but he did not consider what may be happening to them there. The conditions in the upper atmosphere are very different to that at ground level because the radiation from the Sun is much more intense. In 1974, three scientists from Michigan University (Ralph Cicerone, Richard Sytolarski and Stacy Waters) suggested that the CFCs were being broken down by ultraviolet (UV) light and the chlorine atoms that were formed were attacking the ozone molecules. One chlorine atom could destroy millions of ozone molecules before the chain reaction stopped. The delicate balance which kept the amount of ozone in the upper atmosphere constant was being disturbed. The three scientists thought that matters would become serious by the mid-1980s.

Arguments followed in all the scientific magazines but no conclusions were reached and no action taken. Then in 1982, British scientists in the Antarctic took measurements that showed that there was less ozone in the upper atmosphere than there had once been. Since then, American aircraft have been mapping the ozone in the atmosphere

Ozone – the deadly protector

Ozone (O_3) is a reactive, poisonous gas. It is formed in the atmosphere at ground level by car exhausts and industrial fumes. It is a serious pollutant causing breathing problems; it also attacks rubber and plastics. Ozone is also formed and broken down in the upper atmosphere by natural processes. This results in UV light from the Sun being converted into heat. UV light would cause skin cancers and also damage plants, particularly crops, if it reached the ground. We hence want to avoid ozone at ground level, but rely on the high-level ozone to protect us from the UV radiation.

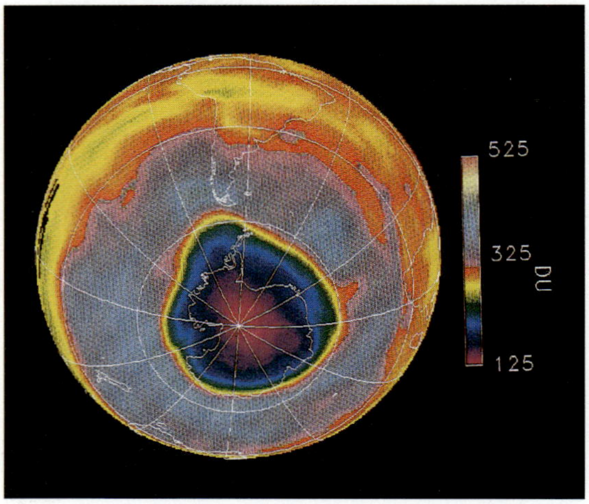

▲ **Measurements taken from space have shown there to be a gap in the ozone layer over the Antarctic**

Now try these

1 CFCs replaced ammonia in refrigerators. Why were CFCs 'better'?

2 Why did scientists disagree about the effect of CFCs in the 1970s?

3 Why did governments not react at once to the news of the hole in the ozone layer over the Antarctic?

4 WP Do people understand the dangers of CFCs? Carry out a survey asking family and friends what they know and understand about CFCs, ozone and the effects of the thinning of the ozone layer?

5 What are shops doing to protect the ozone layer? Are they selling only ozone-friendly goods and are people buying them?

above the South Pole. Every spring the drop in ozone has got more and more worrying. Air over the northern hemisphere has also been found to have reduced ozone.

At last governments took notice, conferences were arranged and agreements made. MacDonalds gave up using CFC-blown takeaway cartons, supermarkets began to stock ozone-friendly aerosols. Nevertheless, the CFCs remain in our fridges and fire extinguishers and will be released into the atmosphere unless they are disposed of carefully. It will be ten years or more before all countries give up using the ozone-destroying CFCs. Will the ozone last that long?

Global warming – myth or reality?

Most of the radiation that reaches the Earth from the Sun is reflected back out into space. This keeps the Earth's climate constant although it varies a great deal from place to place. A slight change in the amount of heat retained by the Earth could cause a great change – or could it?

It has been known since the 1890s that carbon dioxide gas absorbs infra-red light. The Earth radiates most of the Sun's energy back into space as infra-red radiation. So any increase in the amount of carbon dioxide in the atmosphere will mean that more of the Sun's energy is trapped in the atmosphere – the **greenhouse effect**. Methane, nitrogen oxides and CFCs are also 'greenhouse gases', and water was recognised as a greenhouse gas in the middle of the nineteenth century. However, carbon dioxide is the most important as so much is produced by the burning of fossil fuels. The amount of carbon dioxide in the atmosphere has been steadily increasing since the start of the Industrial Revolution in the eighteenth century.

Is the increasing amount of carbon dioxide in the atmosphere affecting the Earth's climate? In the 1930s, some scientists thought it was, because the average air temperature had risen slightly. This was a time of droughts such as the one that caused the Dust Bowl in the USA. Between 1940 and 1970, however, the temperature fell a little and the greenhouse effect was forgotten. In the 1960s and 1970s there was a great expansion in the use of coal and oil all over the world, and scientists observed a steady rise in the amount of carbon dioxide in the atmosphere. The 1980s saw some of the warmest years on record and the greenhouse effect and global warming hit the news.

In Europe, scientists have persuaded governments that global warming is a serious problem. They believe that temperatures are likely to rise in the next few decades and that this will produce changes in the climate. Immediate action must therefore be taken to reduce the use of fossil fuels. In the USA, however, the President is still asking for more surveys and research to be done before a clear conclusion can be reached. It looks likely that we shall just have to wait and see what happens!

Activity

- How do external conditions affect the growth of plants?

You will need: Cress seeds, cotton wool, test tubes and bungs, water bath, a source of carbon dioxide gas.

Plan and carry out an experiment to see how the germination and growth of cress is affected by temperature and the amount of carbon dioxide in the air.

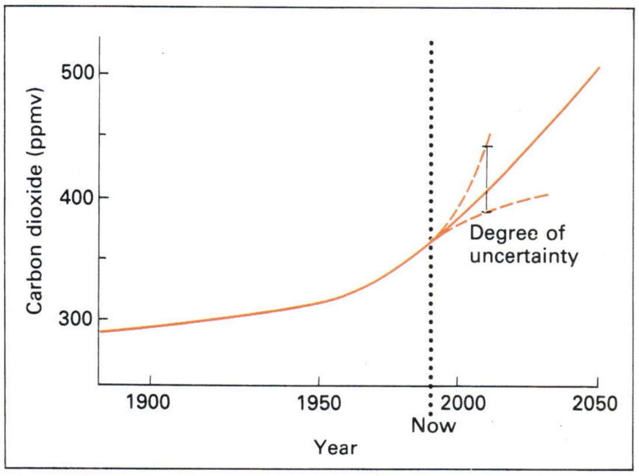

▲ **The increase in carbon dioxide gas in the Earth's atmosphere**

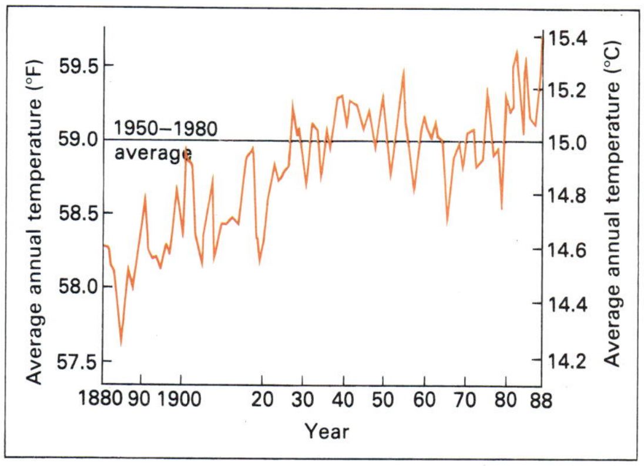

▲ **The increase in the average annual global temperature**

Now try these

1. Discuss whether the decision by European countries to act while collecting data on climates, or the USA's policy of waiting for more information, is most sensible.
2. What are the 'best' alternatives to using fossil fuels for electricity generation and transport?

3.2 TAKING RISKS

We take risks every day in everything we do, eat, drink, watch or travel in. Estimating and measuring risk is now an important role of the statistician in government, industry and the military. How are risks measured and how do the risks of some activities compare with others?

Activity

To estimate risks that people face you need information. Prepare a questionnaire to ask friends, family and anybody else who might take part in your survey.

You need to ask questions like: do they smoke; drink alcohol; ride a bike, motorcycle or drive a car; do they travel on trains, ships or planes; have they suffered from any diseases (cancer, heart disease, lung infections) or allergies (including asthma); have they been involved in any accidents, at home, on the roads, or when travelling on other forms of transport. You need to question as many different people as possible.

Present your findings in a suitable graphical form and then estimate the risk of various things happening. For example, if ten people say they drive cars and two have had accidents then the risk of a road accident is approximately one in five, 20% or 0.2.

- Why are your findings likely to be unreliable?

▲ Is this a greater risk than this? ▼

Daily disasters

Earthquakes in Iran and San Francisco, floods in Bangladesh, aeroplane crashes, motorway pile-ups; these types of disasters regularly appear on the front pages of national newspapers and on national television news. Why? Is it just because of the large loss of life or because they provide an instant story and pictures? Yet as the graph shows, some of the biggest risks to life are smoking, influenza and road accidents (**Note:** the shorter the bar, the greater the risk). These risks cause deaths every day of the year. We are very selective in the risks that we worry about. Yet it is these risks that insurance companies consider when working out the payments for motor insurance, life assurance and other forms of insurance.

It has become very popular in recent years for the media to create scares when scientists have discovered how risky something is, such as BSE in beef, salmonella in eggs, faulty microwave ovens, radiation from computer screens and artificial colours in foods. While undoubtedly there is a risk associated with these things, it is important to note the size of the risk and remember that one thing is certain in the science of risk - nothing is certain.

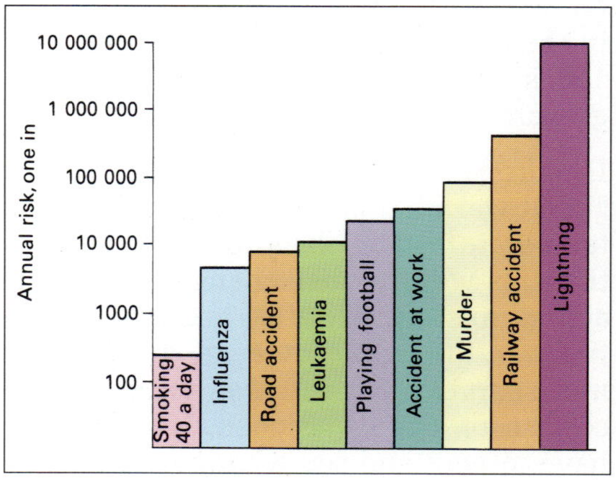

▲ The risk of dying from some of the more common causes

A matter of opinion

While the risks from smoking are easy to calculate as they happen all the time, industry is more concerned with estimating the risks of accidents which they hope will never happen. However, here there is the possibility for lots of disagreement and even the manipulation of figures to produce the answer that you want. One of the biggest differences in opinion has occurred over the risk of nuclear power.

Nuclear reactors were first used for generating electricity in the 1950s, and during the 1960s and 1970s the nuclear industry grew rapidly in the USA, Europe and the USSR. Although building nuclear power stations was expensive, nuclear power was thought to be cheap to produce. It would also provide an alternative to fossil fuels. The developed countries stockpiled uranium very quickly so that nuclear power could give them the possibility of a guarantee of energy, regardless of politics in the Middle East and other oil-producing nations. From the start, however, groups protested against the use of nuclear power. They were worried about the safety of nuclear power stations and the processing of fuel and waste. The protesters talked of horrific accidents causing nuclear explosions and 'meltdowns' that would devastate the country. Nuclear scientists replied that risks of an accident were one in ten million, but even this caused worries. Nuclear power stations are designed with safety in mind. Every piece of machinery is checked for reliability and there are usually back-ups and fail-safe devices to prevent a minor problem becoming a disaster. But scientists know that you can never be totally confident that an accident won't happen - the risk can never be zero. A serious accident at Windscale in 1957 proved this, but it was hushed up by the British government. More people were aware of the accident at Three Mile Island in the USA. Here, a failure of a valve and a poor response by the operators resulted in an escape of radioactive gas within the building containing the reactor. The reactor had to be shut down completely, but no radioactivity escaped and no-one was hurt.

The biggest blow to the nuclear industry was the Chernobyl disaster which spread high-level radiation over a large area of the USSR and even produced radioactive fallout in parts of North Wales and Cumbria. The effects are expected to last for decades. Despite western governments pleading that such a disaster could never happen to their type of nuclear reactors, confidence in nuclear power was shattered. Re-examination of the costs of nuclear power has since practically halted the growth of nuclear power in Britain.

Anti-nuclear protesters are also worried about the risks from radiation emitted from power stations and reprocessing plants every day. In some parts of the country, cases of leukaemia seem to form clusters and there is some evidence that these occur around nuclear plants. Nuclear scientists insist that the radiation given out by these plants is far less than the average background radiation from rocks and cosmic rays, yet the protesters say that the power stations produce an unacceptable risk. Is the risk worth taking in order to have a source of power independent of fossil fuels?

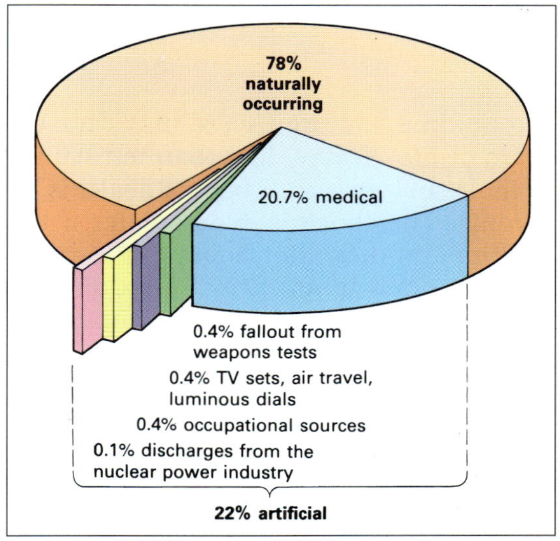

▲ **Average radiation dose for people in the UK**

Radiation dangers

A great deal is known about the effects of a high level of radiation on the human body. Very little is known about the effects of the small amount of radiation that all of us experience from day to day. The nuclear industry sets 'safe' limits for its workers but some scientists now think that there is no level of radiation that does not have some effect on the human body. However as the pie-chart shows, most radiation comes from natural sources which we can do nothing about. A great deal of the artificial radiation comes from medical sources. Doctors now restrict the use of X-rays as there is no doubt that their use carries a risk of cancer. Only a tiny amount of the radiation comes from nuclear power. Is that the whole story or is this type of radiation concentrated in certain places or more dangerous?

Now try these

1 Flying is safer than train or road when the risk is worked out in deaths per passenger mile. Is this a fair comparison? Would it be better to compare deaths per hour of travel or deaths per journey?

2 Supporters of nuclear power say there is more risk in the production of electricity by coal or oil. What are these risks?

3 Are you for or against nuclear power? Give reasons for your answer.

3.3 DEAD IN THEIR SLEEP

At one time, children were lucky to survive their first few years of life. Today, less than ten babies in a thousand die in their first year so a baby's death is a great shock to parents. The shock is even greater if the baby is apparently healthy and dies after being put to bed for a normal night's sleep. Sudden Infant Death Syndrome (SIDS) (also known as cot death) is responsible for a quarter of all deaths of babies under a year old.

Cause of death

When parents find that their baby has died they usually call a doctor. If the doctor is unable to decide immediately why the baby has died he has to inform the Coroner who will order a pathologist to examine the baby. The police usually call to ask some questions. When the Coroner has received the pathologist's report and the police report he must decide whether to issue a death certificate which will allow the baby's funeral to take place or to call an inquest where the evidence will be heard in court.

Sometimes the pathologist will find something wrong with the baby that had not been noticed while the baby was alive. Very often, however, the pathologist will be unable to find an explanation for the cause of death. In these cases he will say the cause of death was SIDS.

Getting to the root of the problem

While SIDS may appear on a baby's death certificate, it is not an explanation of why the baby actually died. Really, it is a recognition that at present we don't know why some babies die in their sleep. Scientists are faced with the problem of trying to find reasons for SIDS and this is difficult since the babies apparently have nothing wrong with them. Scientists have tackled the problem in two different ways. First, they have tried to discover as much as they could about the babies that have died - their age, sex, time of death, previous illnesses, how they lay in their cots, how they were wrapped up - and compared them with normal babies, statistically. Second, researchers have followed up ideas by investigating chemical or biological differences in babies that die suddenly.

Over the last 20 years, scientists have found a few causes of death which were previously unknown. Now when babies die with these disorders they are not classed as SIDS. Of the thousand or so babies who still die from SIDS each year scientists agree that there are probably many reasons for the cause of death.

Research is continuing and most of it in this country is funded by a charity, the Foundation for the Study of Infant Deaths (FSID).

Activity

Look at the graphs below. What conclusions can be drawn from these statistics? Write a report of your findings.

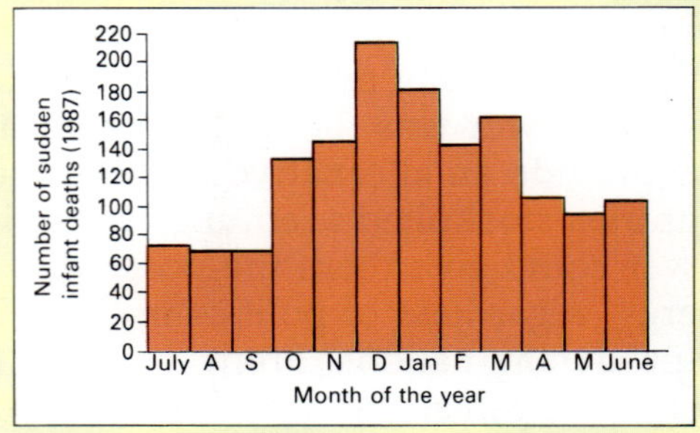

▲ **The number of SIDS per month in 1987**

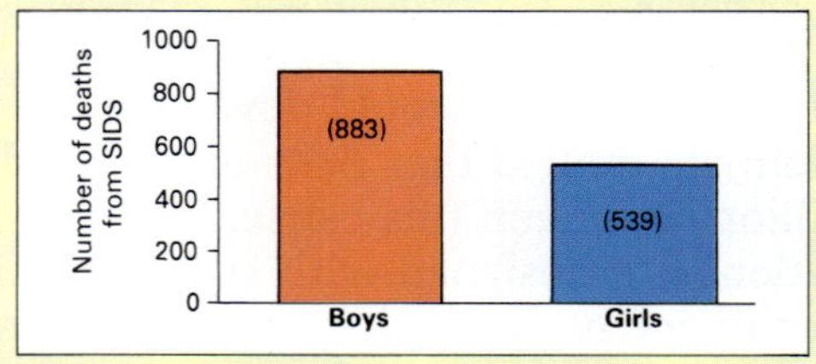

▲ **Deaths from SIDS in 1988**

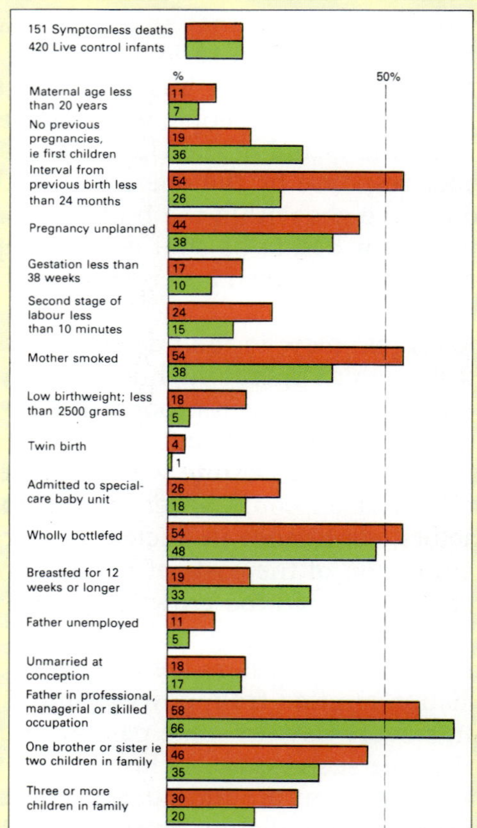

▲ **Characteristics of babies who died from SIDS compared with those of surviving babies**

Lots of theories – little proof

Scientists have put forward many theories for the cause of SIDS. It is important to realise that in this case more than one theory is likely to be correct and the scientists are not competing with one another to find the one and only correct answer. All the different theories discussed here could be true for some of the cases of SIDS.

Enzyme deficiency

Our bodies use hundreds of chemicals to catalyse the reactions necessary for maintaining our life processes. One enzyme in the liver breaks down fats to supply an extra source of energy. Some SIDS babies have been found to have different levels of fats in their livers. This suggests a deficiency of this enzyme.

Smothering

It has been known for mothers to smother their babies for one reason or another. Some doctors think up to 10% of all SIDS deaths may be due to smothering, but other studies have shown that only about 2% of SIDS deaths were suspicious.

Unfortunately some newspapers have given publicity to this as a cause of infant deaths and this has upset many parents of SIDS babies.

Hyperthermia

In cold weather it is natural to want to wrap a baby up in warm blankets. Unfortunately, it seems that this sometimes causes the baby's body temperature to rise too high and result in death.

Apparently babies who sweat a lot are more likely to suffer from this.

Vaccination

Babies are vaccinated to prevent a number of different diseases. It is sometimes thought that the shock of a vaccination may cause SIDS but in fact SIDS is less common in babies that have been vaccinated than in those that have not been.

Sleeping position

Some scientists have found that more SIDS babies were lying on their stomachs than on their backs. It is possible that when lying on their stomachs, babies are unable to push their bedclothes away. However, there is not enough data at the moment to prove the theory.

Mattresses

Some mattresses, particularly old ones made from PVC, give off fumes. It is thought that these fumes may irritate the babies and cause a blockage in their nasal passages.

Infection

Pathologists have often found that SIDS babies have suffered from mild infections. While on their own these infections wouldn't normally kill a baby, it is thought that they might cause the baby to stop breathing.

Breathing control

Breathing is something we rarely think about, but the brain's control of breathing only develops fully during the first year of life. Normally, a baby wakes up if it stops breathing, but in SIDS cases this may not happen. Research is continuing to locate the chemicals involved which stop the brain from stimulating the breathing process.

Now try these

1. Choose one of the theories of the cause of SIDS and plan a study that you could do to test it.
2. What difficulties do researchers face in trying to find the cause of SIDS?
3. If one of the theories were proved to be a cause of SIDS would that mean that the other theories were incorrect? Explain your answer?
4. The Foundation for the Study of Infant Deaths has funded nearly 100 projects since it was formed 20 years ago; most of these have carried out scientific research into the cause of SIDS. Why is it important for many different scientists to continue this research?

If you would like to find out more information about SIDS, or make a donation, the Foundation for the Study of Infant Deaths is at: 15 Belgrave Square, London, SW1X 8PS.

3.4 HIGH OCTANE!

In recent years, there has been a campaign to stop the use of leaded petrol. Campaigners say that leaded petrol pollutes the environment and they have urged car drivers to use the 'green' alternative. Why is lead added to petrol anyway? What evidence is there that lead is a pollutant?

Leaded or unleaded? Does it make a difference?

Activity

Lead is one metal that has been known for thousands of years. Many uses have been found for the metal and its compounds, eg the metal is used in the alloys pewter and solder, it is used on roofs and used to be used for water pipes; lead compounds are also used in some paints and glazes on pottery. It has also been known for a long time that lead compounds are poisonous. Find out some of the properties of lead and its compounds by carrying out the following experiments.

You will need: Test tubes, dropper, pieces of lead, lead nitrate solution, hydrochloric acid, sodium hydroxide solution, sodium chloride solution, sodium iodide solution, sodium chromate solution.

1. Add a few pieces of lead to about 2 cm^3 of hydrochloric acid. Where do you think lead comes in the reactivity table?
2. Place about 2 cm^3 of lead nitrate solution in each of four test tubes. Add a few drops of either sodium hydroxide, sodium chloride, sodium iodide or sodium chromate solution to each and note what happens. What reactions have occurred?

Write up a report on what you have observed.

Why is there lead in petrol?

During World War I there was a great growth in the number of vehicles that ran on petrol. However, the petrol that was available was not refined very well from crude oil and produced 'knocking' in the engines. Knocking occurs when the petrol and air is being compressed in the cylinder and ignites before the spark has been made. This causes the piston to jerk in the cylinder and can damage the engine if it happens too often; it also wastes petrol. In the 1920s, oil companies soon started to add tetra ethyl lead to their petrol. As an additional benefit, it was found that the lead also protected the valves in the engines from wear.

When the petrol is burnt in the engine, 99% of the tetra ethyl lead breaks down. Most of it is exhausted as lead oxide; some is trapped in the exhaust. It has been found that most lead is exhausted when the engine is cold and when the car is accelerating, while comparatively little is given out when a car travels at constant motorway speeds.

THOMAS MIDGLEY
1889–1944

Thomas was born in Pennsylvania, USA, the son of an engineer. He studied mechanical engineering at Cornell University and then worked on torpedoes during early World War I. In 1916, he joined the Dayton Engineering Company and started research on knocking in petrol engines. He tested many different substances as anti-knock agents before discovering the properties of tetra ethyl lead. He became a vice-president of the Ethyl Corporation in 1923 (the Corporation became part of the Dow Chemical Company). In 1930, he introduced freon, the first of the CFCs, as a refrigerant. Freon rapidly replaced the use of ammonia and chloro-methane which had been found to be poisonous. In 1940, Thomas became paralysed by polio and died in Ohio in 1944. It is ironic that the two substances for which Midgley is famous and which were thought to be of great benefit to people, are now considered to be a great danger to the environment.

Lead and you

Lead is not a rare element and we encounter it every day.

- **Food** - plants absorb lead compounds from the soil and animals eat plants containing lead. We normally 'eat' about 100 μg a day (a μg is one millionth of a gram, a micro-gram), but most of this is excreted.
- **Water** - water usually only contains a tiny amount of lead, but some water sources originate in areas contaminated by lead ores. Lead pipes are now being replaced as it is recognised that they can contaminate water.
- **Air** - the lead from petrol gets into the air that we breathe. An experiment in Turin found that about 25% of the lead in people's bodies came from the lead used in petrol. In rural areas only about 12% of body lead was found to come from petrol.

Lead can penetrate all parts of our bodies. After being given a dose of lead, it takes the blood about one month to reduce the level by half, a few months for the brain and other soft tissues, but ten years for the lead in bones to drop by 50%.

It has been known since ancient times that a high dose of lead is poisonous and can kill. A level of over 90 μg of lead per 100 ml of blood causes an inflammation of the brain that leads to seizures and brain damage. This level is very rare but it can be caused by inhaling the fumes from leaded petrol for long periods. At levels below 90 μg/100 ml, the effects are much more difficult to measure.

IQ and lead – the evidence

The earliest investigation into the effects of lead was in 1943 when Byers and Lord followed the progress of 20 children who had high levels of lead in their bodies, but were apparently healthy. They were found to have difficulty with school work. In 1963, Smith measured the IQ of a group of children with high lead levels. Their average IQ was 87 whereas the national average is about 100. However, other research failed to repeat these results. A survey in London of children who lived near a lead-smelting works found that the average IQ was the same as that of childen who lived elsewhere.

Then in 1972, De La Burde and Choate compared 70 children with an average of 58 μg lead/100 ml blood with 72 children with much lower lead levels. The low-lead children had an average IQ five points better than that of the high-lead children. In 1974, Rummo found similar results with 44 children who had varying levels of lead in their bodies.

These results convinced many people that above-average levels of lead in children caused reduced intelligence but it has been difficult to prove. Some children from badly contaminated areas in Birmingham did better in exams than expected.

Campaign for lead-free petrol

In Britain, the organisation CLEAR campaigned for many years for the removal of lead from petrol. In the late 1980s, oil companies began to sell unleaded petrol and most new cars now use it. Since World War II, the refining of oil has improved and petrol companies can now provide petrol without any additives that does not cause knocking. Indeed the amount of lead in leaded petrol reduced from 0.84 g/l in 1970 to 0.15 g/l in 1985.

In the USA, unleaded petrol had been compulsory since the mid-1970s. This is not because of the fear of lead poisoning, but because campaigns against the other pollutants produced by burning petrol have resulted in all cars being fitted with catalytic convertors (cats). As lead would damage the cats, the cars must run on unleaded fuel. Cats are not yet common in Britain.

Now try these

1. Why have high lead levels been found in children living near Spaghetti Junction in Birmingham? (Spaghetti Junction is where a number of busy roads and motorways meet.)
2. Were oil companies right to use Midgley's discovery of lead anti-knock agents?
3. Do you think it has been proved that lead in petrol causes children to be less intelligent? Explain your answer.
4. Carry out a survey to find what percentage of cars are now using unleaded fuel.

3.5 THE RACE INTO SPACE

It is difficult to imagine the world today without its space industries. We have come to expect instant television pictures from all over the world, easy telephone links to everywhere, weather forecasts that show satellite photographs of Britain, and the exciting data revealed by pictures from *Voyager* and *Giotto* about our Solar System.

Rockets in space

Robert Godard in the USA and Konstantin Tsiolkovsky in the USSR began the modern science of rocketry with work on controllable liquid-fuelled rockets in the early twentieth century. Their work found its first use in World War II when Herman Oberth designed and built the V2 missile for Germany. After the war, the German rocket scientists dispersed, some to the USA and some to the USSR. Werner von Braun, one of Oberth's assistants, was to lead the American rocket programme, but it was the Soviets who got into space first with *Sputnik 1* in October 1957. *Sputnik* was simply a radio transmitter and performed no other purpose than to show that launching a satellite into space was possible. The Americans soon followed, but the Soviets scored another first in April 1961 when Yuri Gagarin became the first person to travel in space.

Cold war competition

What was the purpose of these early flights into space? Undoubtedly many of the engineers working on the space programmes in both countries were fired by the challenge to bring to life the science fiction stories of space travel. However, the governments supported the programmes because of fear and pride. Rockets could carry bombs as well as satellites, and during the 1950s and 1960s there was a great fear that either the USA or the USSR would start World War III. Each country hence wanted to ensure that it had the most advanced weapons. Even though war did not break out, each country tried to prove that its technology was the best.

In 1963, while the Russians still apparently led the space race, President Kennedy of the USA stated that America would put a man on the Moon before the end of the decade. With the voyage of *Apollo 11* in 1969, that objective was achieved and the space race was won. The Soviets declared that they had never been in the race, although it seems that plans had been made for a Soviet Moon flight. Their program was delayed until it was too late to beat the Americans. There was no propaganda in coming second. The Moon race was expensive both in terms of money and lives. The USA lost three astronauts who were killed in a fire on the launch pad, while Vladimir Komarov died when

Activity

1. The Space Shuttle often carries experiments to investigate the effects of weightless conditions on plants, animals and even chemical reactions like crystallisation and polymerisation. Plan an experiment to be carried out in space to test the effects of weightlessness.
2. The Viking lander on Mars carried an experiment to discover if there was any signs of life in the Martian soil. Plan an experiment that could achieve this.

■ What's beneath the Venusian atmosphere?

The American *Mariner* and *Magellan* and the Soviet *Venera* craft mapped the dry, hot surface.

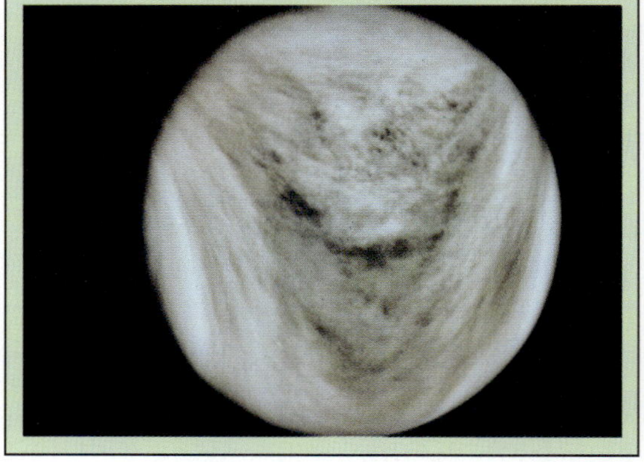

■ How were Saturn's rings formed?

The *Voyager* craft sent back detailed photographs showing that the rings were far more complicated than first thought.

his parachute failed to open. Risks were taken. In order to achieve publicity, the Soviets packed three men into a one-man *Vostok* craft without space suits, parachutes, ejector seats or reserve oxygen supplies.

Science in space

While the governments competed, scientists and engineers made the most of the space programmes. Uncrewed space craft were sent to the Moon, Mars and Venus to collect dat for astronomers. More and more satellites went into orbit around the Earth. Many were intended to provide better communications as foreseen by Arthur C. Clarke in 1945. Others send back data about the Earth's atmosphere and surface. These satellites give important information about weather patterns and the state of vegetation all over the Earth. Similar satellites also spy on military movements in various countries.

Having lost the race to the Moon, the Soviets concentrated on launching the space stations, *Salyut* and *Mir*, which have been occupied by cosmonauts for periods of nearly a year. This has told us a lot about how the human body is affected by space travel.

From the start of the space programme to the flights of the Shuttle, scientists have been searching for new materials to cope with conditions in space and on re-entry into the Earth's atmosphere. Solar cells have been steadily improved to provide more power for less weight and engineers have found ways of lightening rockets so that they can carry a greater payload. Much of this research has eventually found its way into other industries.

The new race – make it pay

Countries all over the world want satellites to be launched for a variety of reasons. Building satellites has become a lucrative business for companies such as British Aerospace. Competition has now arisen for the launch of the satellites. The European Space Associations built its *Ariane* rockets to compete with the Americans and Soviets, and China and Japan are not far behind. Satellite Television is the latest business to try to make money out of space and people are now being persuaded to buy satellite dishes which will receive TV pictures from all over the world.

Has it been worth it? Would the money spent on space exploration have been better spent on aid to developing countries or to help solve environmental problems? Do countries benefit from improved communications, navigation, weather forecasting and early warnings of pests affecting crops? What have scientists learnt from the various uncrewed space probes – *Surveyors, Mariners, Vikings, Voyagers, Giotto, Hipparcos,* and many others?

■ Are comets dirty snowballs?

Giotto showed that Halley's comet was mainly ice, but what was the dark covering on the peanut-shaped core?

■ How was the Moon formed?

Samples of Moon rock brought back by the *Apollo* astronauts revealed that the Moon was not once part of the Earth. This question has never fully been answered though.

Now try these

1 Which of the following do you think are sensible uses for space satellites? Explain your answers for each.

- communications
- satellite TV
- weather forecasting
- Earth resources and crop monitoring
- military intelligence
- astronomy
- research for new industries (eg zero-gravity drug manufacture).

2 The exploration of space has provided some answers but has also prompted more questions. Why do you think this has happened?

3 Uncrewed space probes are a lot cheaper than crewed space missions. Do you think that there should be a crewed space programme? Explain your answer.

3.6 MISTAKES AND FAKES

If you have read through this book and *What is Science*? you will have discovered that science today is the result of work by many men and women from different times, cultures and backgrounds. What have they been trying to do? Many scientists will say that they are trying to find the truth about the Universe, but how do we or they know what the truth is? How can we be certain that science is correct? The answer is that we can't, but over the centuries scientists and philosophers have tried to come up with a 'method' which will ensure that science is correct.

Galileo was the first to describe a scientific method. He said that experiment and observation could be used to *prove* laws and theories devised by the scientist. The philosopher, Karl Popper, has now turned that method on its head. He proposes that experiments are used to *disprove* theories and that it is impossible to prove a theory once and for all. The American philosopher, Thomas Kuhn, says that scientists tend to work with an accepted set of laws and theories, steadily acquiring more knowledge until contradictions suddenly appear. The accepted theories then undergo a 'revolution'. Revolutions in science occurred in seventeenth-century astronomy when Copernicus' theory of the Universe replaced the theory that the Earth was at the centre of the Universe. In the eighteenth century, Lavoisier's Oxygen Theory changed chemists' ideas on combustion and this century the Quantum Theory changed physicists' view of the behaviour of particles.

Scientists are ordinary people. They may have bright ideas or be excellent experimenters but they also suffer from pride, jealousy, greed, and envy. This has resulted in some episodes in the history of science that now seem far-fetched and laughable. Scientists have also been driven into faking proof of their theories in order to gain support.

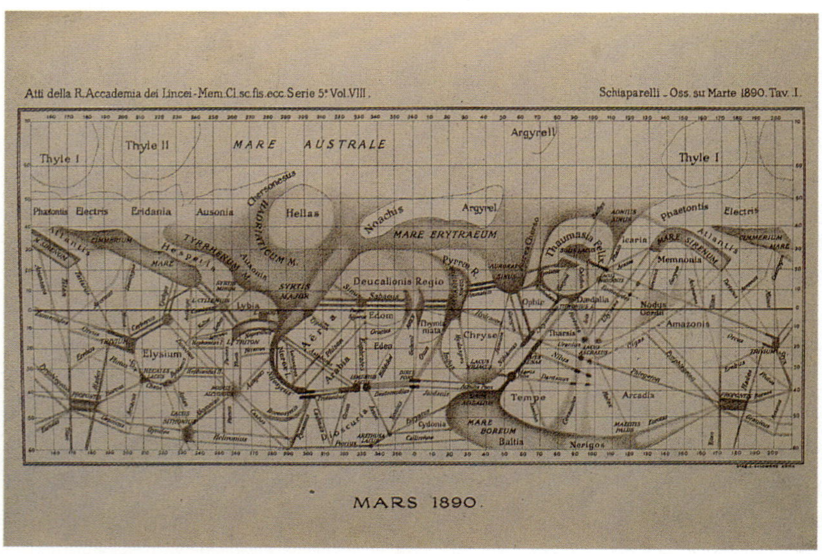

▲ **Is this what Schiaparelli and Lowell saw?**

Activity

Proof or disproof?

Devise experiments to test the folowing hypotheses:

1 *'Energy cannot be created or destroyed but just changed from one form to another.'*

- What different forms of energy are there?

2 *'When the Moon is between the Sun and the Earth a spring tide is produced.'*

- What is a spring tide?

3 *'The melting point of a hydrocarbon is determined by the length of its carbon chain.'*

- What are the first six alkanes called?

Is it possible to *prove* these hypotheses? Are other factors involved which might explain your observations?

MARTIAN WATERWORKS

Before Galileo, the Universe above the Earth was thought to be perfect while only the Earth could be inhabited by imperfect humans. Galileo observed that the Moon and the planets were similar to the Earth and he even suggested that there might be life on the Moon. Later astronomers tended to agree with him. In 1877, the Italian Giovanni Schiaparelli observed straight lines on the surface of Mars which he called *canali*, meaning 'channels'. Unfortunately the word was translated as 'canals' and many people assumed them to be waterways. The American astronomer Percival Lowell also observed the 'canals' and alleged that they had been built by Martians to carry water from the poles to the desert areas. Although other astronomers failed to see the canals, the idea became popular and gave authors like H. G. Wells, Edgar Rice Burroughs and Ray Bradbury material for their Martian stories. As late as the 1930s, there was still popular belief in the Martian canals although improved telescopes failed to observe them. In the 1960s and 1970s, the *Mariner* and *Viking* space probes revealed Mars as a dry, dead planet with no sign of grand artificial waterways, although there were signs of dried-up river canyons.

Radio waves, X-rays, γ-rays – and *N-rays*?

The last 20 years of the nineteenth century saw many discoveries of different types of energy produced as rays. In 1888, Heinrich Herz discovered radio waves; in 1895, Wilhelm Röntgen discovered X-rays and the radioactivity discovered by Henri Becquerel in 1896 was found by Ernest Rutherford to be made up of α, β and γ radiation. Then in 1903, the French physicist, Blondlot, discovered **N-rays**. He proposed that N-rays were given off when substances were heated or stressed (such as tempered steel), and by living things. Like X-rays they passed through solid objects and disturbed sparks. They also had the property of aiding vision so that people could see things in a darkened room. Blondlot who had already made a name for himself by proving that X-rays travelled at the speed of light, reported his observations to the French Academie des Sciences. During the summer and autumn of 1903 a number of other French scientists confirmed his results. However, Ernest Rutherford failed to find any evidence for N-rays and J. J. Thompson, who had discovered the electron, said it was all in Blondlot's imagination. In September 1904, Blondlot gave a demonstration to an audience. In the darkened room, Blondlot produced a beam of N-rays. Unknown to him, however, a member of the audience moved a prism that was supposed to be refracting the rays but this apparently had no effect on the beam. Then the spectator replaced an iron bar, which an assistant was using to 'see' a clock, with a piece of wood. The assistant's improved sight was not affected. Blondlot's demonstrations were shown to be all his imagination and his N-rays a mere illusion.

▲ **Small apparatus, big fuss!**

Fusion confusion

In March 1989, newspapers around the world carried news of a miraculous discovery. Stanley Pons and Martin Fleischmann had announced cold fusion. They had passed an electric current between a platinum and palladium electrode, through deuterium oxide (heavy water) and produced a great amount of heat. They thought the heat must be due to the fusion of deuterium atoms into helium. Their announcement was unusual for two reasons. First, billions of pounds had been spent on projects to produce cheap power from this process, yet Pons and Fleischmann had announced that it could be done with simple apparatus in an ordinary laboratory. Second, scientists usually announce their results in magazines read only by other scientists. Pons and Fleischmann announced their results in a blaze of publicity.

Over the next few months, teams of scientists tried to copy Pons and Fleischmann's results. Steven Jones had been working on a similar cold-fusion process but disagreed with the huge amount of energy that Pons and Fleischmann said they had produced. Some scientists said that Pons and Fleischmann had used faulty equipment, made mistakes in calculations or failed to control some factors. The story faded out of the newspapers.

Now try these

1. Why was there uncertainty about Schiaparelli's and Lowell's observations?
2. Why do you think Blondlot's N-rays were accepted by French scientists at first?
3. Why do you think many scientists were unhappy about the way that Pons and Fleischmann publicised their 'discovery'.
4. See if you can find any other examples of theories which were accepted for a short time before being discredited.

3.6 MISTAKES AND FAKES

Training fakers

Have you ever fiddled, cooked, made up or otherwise faked results for a school science experiment? Don't be afraid to admit it, because most scientists have done the same thing. Experiments done in school are often rushed, so that there is little opportunity to repeat measurements or check doubtful ones. Also there is always a large element of experimental error due to poorly cleaned or maintained apparatus and inexpert pupils. Unfortunately, there are very many examples of scientists, young and old, who have been lured into the trap of publishing results that they have made up. Why do they do it?

Scientists gain promotion and good research jobs only if they make a name for themselves by publishing papers in academic magazines. Although these papers are read by referees, the experiments are not, and often cannot be, repeated to check results. If the referee approves, the paper will be published. When the scientist wants money for his research, his work is examined by other scientists working in the same subject. They will look at the papers the scientist has written and judge the value of the work that has been done. So it is relatively easy for faked results to be accepted. Young scientists doing their first research, after obtaining a degree, are supervised by older scientists. However, the supervisors are often busy with their own work and cannot check every single experiment that the young researcher does.

Is faked science important? It is said that science is searching for the **truth** about the Universe. Hence, faking knowledge goes against every objective of scientists. More important, in today's world, society depends on scientists to provide answers to problems. Just one news story that a scientist has faked results will add to the distrust that some people already feel regarding science.

Past masters of fakery

There is nothing new in faking scientific results. Many famous scientists in history have faked results and they often weren't revealed as fakers for hundreds of years. They used all the methods of fakery that are used today!

Making up results: One of Galileo's most famous pieces of research was to roll balls down a slope to test the law of motion of falling bodies. Galileo described the results of 'hundreds of experiments' and they fitted his law very well. Scientists in Italy at the time failed to get as good results from their experiments. It is now thought that despite his enthusiasm for experiment, Galileo probably made up his results. Galileo's law is correct, so long as there is no friction to hinder the ball's progress down the slope.

Activity

The formula of magnesium oxide

This is a common experiment in school chemistry courses, designed to illustrate Dalton's Law of Multiple Proportions.

You will need: Magnesium, crucible and lid, tripod and crucible support, Bunsen burner, accurate balance.

First, weigh the crucible empty; then weigh it again with a small piece of magnesium. Place the crucible containing magnesium, with its lid, on the tripod and heat strongly for at least five minutes. You will need to lift the lid off now and again to let air in. Allow the crucible to cool, then weigh it again. Keep heating and cooling the crucible until the mass remains constant.

Calculate the mass of the magnesium and the change in mass after heating. Divide the mass of magnesium by 12 and the change in mass by 16. What is the ratio of these two figures?

The answer should be exactly 1, as the formula of magnesium oxide is MgO. How close was your result? What would you do if you were going to be marked on the accuracy of your result? In fact this experiment is notoriously inaccurate. What sources of error can you think of?

▲ Did Galileo really do this experiment?

Cooking the figures: Isaac Newton's great work *Principia* contains lots of measurements that he made up to support his Laws of Motion and Gravitation.

Newton claimed that his results were accurate to 0.1% and this helped the acceptance of his ideas a great deal. However, it now appears that Newton carefully corrected most of his results in order to achieve that accuracy. It was a couple of hundred years before apparatus improved to the extent that Newton's results could be duplicated.

Being selective: The Manchester chemist, John Dalton, is remembered for his Atomic Theory, part of which was the Law of Multiple Proportions which stated that elements combine in simple ratios to form compounds. He backed up his law with the results of experiments on the oxides of nitrogen (N_2O, NO, NO_2). Dalton's results certainly supported his law but efforts to repeat his experiments have produced many other results which do not. It seems that Dalton simply picked out the results which suited him and ignored the rest.

Stealing results: For 1500 years until Copernicus, Ptolemy's theory of the motion of the planets was accepted by astronomers. In his book known as *Almagest*, Ptolemy claimed to have made measurements of the positions of stars and planets which supported his ideas. Instead, it is apparent that he actually took the observations of the Greek astronomer, Hipparchus, 278 years earlier and calculated where the Sun and the planets would be in his own time. In fact, he had made no observations of his own.

Modern fakers

William Summerlin was one of about 50 researchers working for Robert Good at the Sloan-Kettering Institute for Cancer Research in Manhattan. All the scientists usually added Good's much respected name to their papers, so his name appeared on about 700 papers a year. Summerlin was working on the transplantation of skin and other organs and trying to find ways of overcoming the rejection that usually occurred.

In 1973, Summerlin published a paper along with Good, in which he said that skin kept in nutrient solution for a few days could be transplanted without problems of rejection. He included results of experiments with rabbits to prove it. The story got a lot of publicity because of the help it would give to patients needing skin grafts. However, other scientists couldn't repeat the results and started to question how Summerlin had got them. Eventually, Good himself became worried. To convince him, Summerlin showed him some mice which he said had received skin transplants without any problems. The grafted skin was coloured black while the rest of the mice were white. Good accepted Summerlin's result, but an assistant realised that Summerlin had used a felt-tip pen to produce the black patches. Summerlin was suspended and all his research discarded. Good was rebuked for failing to supervise his workers sufficiently.

■ The skull of Piltdown Man - the earliest inhabitant of Britain. This was in fact a fake that fooled scientists for many years.

The future of science

There is no doubt that science will be as important in the future as it has been in the past. Men and women are needed to solve the puzzles that still exist and to provide answers for the problems that face us and our planet.

The lessons of the past are that we should always question what scientists state as experimental fact or scientific law, that all observations and experimental results must be checked and rechecked, and that there is always uncertainty.

Science can be routine and repetitive but there is always a need for imagination to provide new theories, new ways of experimenting, and to foresee some of the implications of the discoveries that are made.

Now try these

1 Do you think that Galileo and Newton were correct to publish their theories even though they did not really have experimental proof? Explain your answer.

2 Why do you think that the research that scientists publish is rarely repeated?

3 What do you think can and should be done to prevent scientists faking results?

4 Would you fake results to ensure that you kept your job, or to become respected? Think carefully about your answer.

INDEX